I0477493

ISBN: 978-1-796-53855-7

The Older I Get...
...The Smarter
My Dad
Becomes

Life Lessons from a Sales Leadership Legend

"This book offers an intimate expression of the wit and wisdom of one of the most honest, nicest, smartest, funniest, business and sales leaders many of us have ever met. A great read and the next best thing to sitting down with a true legend."

- Joe Buzzello - Founder SELSource.com, Aflac West Territory, Hall of Fame, best selling author: The CAP Equation

"For the new salesperson, this is an inspirational visit to a sprinkling of life's wisdom and gives you an education you can't get in college about being a true entrepreneur. For the veteran salesperson, it's a "way-back" machine to your own memories of how you made the "accidental" career choice of sales. Jimmy Hill touched a multitude of lives that still thrives today through the generations of baton passers. You will thoroughly enjoy reading this book!"

- Ronald Sanders – former Aflac Director of Sales, Aflac Hall of Fame Member.

"I've had the privilege of knowing and working with Jimmy for over 25 years. He and Margaret and the boys are first class Americans all the way. Jimmy's success with Aflac as a team builder, leader and innovator is legendary."

- Michael J. Tomlinson, Retired Sr. V.P., Dir. of U.S. Sales

Foreword

"There's a thin thread that connects people and things to our lives."

—James R. 'Jimmy' Hill

He told me that once.

He went on to say that, "God puts people and things in front of you," and then he wisely advised, "You damn well have to be smart enough to grab ahold of those *right* people and those *right* things at the *right* time."

I met Jimmy, Margaret, Jay and Greg (the Hill family) in Los Angeles in the summer of 1987. I was broke and a bit broken. At twenty-six years old, I'd already experienced a lot of pain. I'd come off a year that would have wiped out the entrepreneurial aspirations of most people. During the previous fourteen months, I'd lost $470,000 of my family's money in a Ponzi scheme, my business and income vaporized, cars were repossessed, my home went into foreclosure, and I declared bankruptcy. While this was occurring, my father was diagnosed with lung cancer and passed away. The final piece of carnage would be the collapse of my young marriage. When the ashes settled, I found myself back in the insurance business, trying to generate enough commission to pay the rent, and put food in the fridge. I was no prize, no candidate that any hiring manager would take a second look at.

At this juncture, the lowest point of my life, I received a phone call from Jimmy Hill's oldest son, Jay. It was a recruiting call. Jay promised that Jimmy would, "buy me lunch." A few days later I was in Torrance, meeting with Jimmy. I almost didn't go to the meeting that day—I was busy and considered calling Jay to cancel—blowing off the lunch because I thought it might be a distraction to my day. But I did go to meet Jimmy that day and he went on to become one of the most important business and personal mentors of my life.

I'm not sure why, but Jimmy decided to hire me. Like I said, I was no prize—most high-level managers wouldn't have pursued me hard or pursued me at all, but he saw something. He gave me a managerial opportunity with a company that would come to be known as Aflac. My relationship (and my road) with Jimmy Hill unwound; taking a few interesting turns and detours. It's funny how things work; in early 1990, I left the company for what I considered to be a "better opportunity." The strange phenomena that next ensued can only be called, "providential."

For some reason, Jimmy stayed in touch with me over the next three years. He even coaxed Jay and Greg to dial me up once in a while. It was like I'd become an unofficial member of the Hill family. When we'd get together, Jimmy would tell me how well "American Family" was doing in Los Angeles, and he'd casually say something like, "timing is everything, Joe."

I recall his foretelling, "Joe, I see you being back with us one day, becoming one of the most successful leaders our company has ever seen, developing great personal wealth. That's what I see in your future." I never knew how to respond to those things when he said them. I think I would simply smile and nod my head.

But my point is, who does that kind of thing?

What manager stays in touch with some loser that left their company—invites them out to dinner? Who keeps in contact with somebody for several years—when they're not part of your business, then prophesizes about his or her future with a company they aren't even with?

I can assure you that NOBODY does that.

But this was Jimmy Hill. He was playing the long game and nobody did it better than Jimmy. He could have easily just forgotten about me when I left. I could have just as easily not accepted any of the social invitations from him. To reflect back on that summer of 1987, it was only the lure of a "free lunch" that shifted my decision to drive down to Torrance to meet with him in the first place.

A "thin thread" for darn sure!

I don't want to keep you in suspense. Jimmy was able to hire me back in 1993. He relished getting me back into the Aflac family and he also used the 'needle' regularly to remind me of my return. From that point on, for years and years (and whenever he had a slightly lubed-up audience), he'd introduce me in the following manner:

"Hey everybody, this is Joe Buzzello. He's so dumb, I had to hire him TWICE!"

He'd deliver this classic Jimmy line, over and over again (usually at the bar) and then he'd wait for the laugh. Then he'd laugh harder than the crowd.

I will add that, behind every successful man…there's usually someone else. In this case that someone else is one Margaret Hill. Margaret reminds me a lot of my mother. I think God broke the mold when He made people like them. Margaret was certainly by Jimmy's side during the good times—the great business growth and success he experienced during his long and illustrious career. Margaret was there to offer guidance, whispering in Jimmy's ear—and sometimes talking a bit louder than a whisper. LOL! I believe that I heard Jimmy refer to Margaret as, "The Boss," on more than one occasion.

Margaret has also been glued to Jimmy's side when times haven't been so good. Time and age catch up to all of us eventually and Father Time can be cruel. I can assure you that Margaret will stay by Jimmy's side, undaunted, doing what she does, offering strength and love. That's what people like her do.

Joe Buzzello and Jimmy Hill

When Greg Hill advised me that he had begun a manuscript that would become this book, I broke out in the hugest smile. While Jimmy has meant so much to me personally, he has also touched so many others. Jimmy's impact on the people that worked with him and around him should not be understated. I don't know of a single man or woman that has met Jimmy that hasn't walked away a better person. He's that kind of unique human being—he's that irreplaceable.

There's no doubt that Greg and the Hill family have completed this book with the help and support of many people that know and love Jimmy. Whether you realize it or not, Greg and the people that contributed to these writings may have just delivered you a very special GIFT. It's not a free lunch and a long friendship with the great Jimmy Hill, but it is the **next best thing**. It's an intimate expression of all of the wit and wisdom of one of the most honest, nicest, smartest, funniest, business and sales leaders many of us have ever met.

For me personally, Jimmy was one of those few "thin threads" that God put in my life. Fortunately, I was "damn well smart enough" to grab ahold of him at the right time. Jimmy and Margaret's love and caring changed everything for me and sent my life on the right trajectory.

So, please…consider this book your gift—your "thin thread" to Jimmy and his experience and knowledge of the world of business, sales and the game of life. God put this book in your hands for some good reason, now simply allow Jimmy's *voice* to sagely advise and guide you.

There is nobody quite like him, and I'm so blessed to have gotten to know him and the Hill family.

Joe Buzzello - Scottsdale Arizona, Spring 2019
Founder, SELSource.com, Aflac, West Territory, Hall of Fame, bestselling author of: *The CAP Equation, Drawing Circles* and *A Life in Sales*

Preface

I've come to realize that writing a book has proven to be a daunting task. Over the years, distractions, procrastination and self-imposed 'writer's block' have combined to derail my numerous attempts at authorship. I'm no different than many budding authors that are full of vigor in the beginning only to find the level of enthusiasm waning as completion seems further out of reach.

I have never considered myself an amazing wordsmith or a seasoned writer possessing a high level of satirical wit. I'm just a guy with a story that I wanted to share with folks that may want to hear it. I sincerely hope that you enjoy my attempt at literary immortality. Hopefully, there may be a few nuggets of wisdom that you may apply to your career or life in general.

There are so many people that helped me in this endeavor and I'd like to take an opportunity to thank a few of them. This list is definitely not all-inclusive and I hope I've not offended anyone with their omission.

First off, I'd like to thank my wife, Liza, for putting up with my numerous crazy ideas over the years. She has been a wonderful partner in tempering my enthusiasm from time to time without quashing my creative urges. Artists can be temperamental and she has an uncanny knack for striking the perfect balance of constructive criticism.

I'd also like to thank my mother, Margaret, and my brother, Jay for proofreading and clarifying some of the stories along with my good friend, Rob Woomer, for his essential blunt appraisals and opinions.

A huge thanks to author and friend, Joe Buzzello. He has served as a great model when crafting the manuscript and has proven to be an invaluable resource in guiding me through this process. I highly recommend his books!

Finally, none of this could have been accomplished without my father, Jimmy Hill. In no way should he be considered just a 'character' in a book. He has inspired many people over the years to 'Go For It" and pursue their dreams. Dad - this book is for you.

I

"Circling"

An Introduction to "Jimmyisms"

The condescending eye roll, followed by the inevitable exhalation accompanied by a smug retort. The complete and utter disbelief that Mom or Dad have even an ounce of intelligence or knowledge about anything.

Every parent of a teenager has probably experienced this at some point or another. We bite our tongues and resist offering a witty retort knowing that it will probably fall on very deaf ears. I typically fail in this attempt usually resulting in yet another eye roll. The cycle is then replayed.

When discussing these encounters with our friends who are also raising teens, my wife and I usually refer to it as "payback" for our naïve misjudgments of our youth. The days in which we, exactly like our own precious offspring, fervently believed that our parents were essentially clueless.

Parents by nature (or requirement) assume many roles for their children. Teacher, Disciplinarian, Mentor. The job, on the surface, is seemingly simple: Equip our kids with the tools needed for them to succeed in this ever changing, competitive world. As any parent can attest: achieving this task is much easier said than done.

I started my career in sales when I was a teenager. My boss was none other than my dad. Yes – the very same person that I could hardly fathom possessed the capacity or common sense to even make it through a typical day. To further challenge my teenage sensibilities, my mom was his unwavering business partner! From my vantage point, a stereophonic cacophony of nonsensical advice spouted from them on a continual basis.

Given my vast experience and exceedingly high level of knowledge of the intricacies needed for a successful career in sales, I did what every other teenage salesperson would do in the same situation; I put on my ear muffs, ignored any parental/boss advice and essentially zoned out. Kinda....

To really understand our family dynamic and how it relates to selling, we should really go back in time to the 1960s. My father, Jimmy, owned a service station in the small town of Louisburg, NC. He was very proud of the fact that his Esso station was always the top franchise in terms of overall sales. He achieved this by creating an exceptional customer experience. He realized that the success of his business was predicated on creating a culture of excellence and pride for and with his employees. Professional, clean uniforms were required. Courteous customer service was required. Attendants (yes, there was a time that this role existed!) were instructed to look for additional motoring needs – windshield wipers, oil changes, new tires, etc. – and inquire if these services could be performed. If a person only required the use of the restroom facilities, their windshields would be cleaned. I'm guessing this is the reason the name has changed from "Service Station" to "Gas Station" over the years! These "Service Attendants" became Salespeople and helped the business flourish.

Jimmy Hill, Esso Station, Louisburg, NC. 1960's

These sales basics were learned from a simple training manual published for Esso franchises in the 1930's by LaSalle Extension University entitled 'Esso Salesmanship'. The book is only 104 pages long and the covered sales techniques remain relevant to this day.

In 1972, disaster struck. Literally. A lightning strike completely burned the service station to the ground. Under-insured and facing financial ruin, my parents made the difficult decision to uproot the family and move to the small county of Buckingham, Virginia. He took a job working for my grandfather's construction company. His dream of owning and running a successful business never subsided, though.

Enter the Multi-Level marketing organization known as Amway. After watching a gentleman "draw circles" describing the fantastic opportunities for wealth accumulation, my parents were all in. My childhood was filled with weekends terrorizing hotels with other kids while our parents attended motivational seminars and conventions. Events were continually held at our house as the Hill organization rapidly expanded. My dad would work his construction job during the day and "sell the Amway dream" to new folks in the evening (usually driving great distances). On the surface, the organization was on a roll! There was one issue though: the promised riches never seemed to appear. Late one evening after his car ended up in a ditch due to a lack of sleep, he came to the realization that a change was overdue.

At some point in life (or usually multiple points), we are forced to make a career defining decision. We make this decision based on all known factors. We thoroughly investigate the potential advantages and disadvantages of our options. We solicit opinions from trusted advisors. My dad made his decision based simply on observing who made the most money in the community.

He determined that the folks that seemed to have the largest houses, drove the nicest cars and seemed to take the best vacations were doctors, lawyers and salespeople. Given his status as a college drop-out with no designs on the continued pursuit of a degree, the first two careers were definitely not options. A career in insurance sales was the obvious choice. There were two major roadblocks: passing the dreaded insurance exam and a speech disorder. He stuttered.

His was not a mild case of stuttering. It was so severe that we would usually have to order dinner at restaurants for him. Introducing himself to others was a struggle. Usually, the ability to effectively communicate (or, at a minimum, be able to explain a product's benefits) is a crucial element to a successful career in sales. To Jimmy, this was simply a minor detail that was easy to overcome. Eventually, he learned to simply coax his customer into reading his sales brochure and have them *"sell themselves the policy."*

The other obstacle known as the "Virginia State Insurance Exam" proved to be more difficult. Multiple attempts at passing this regulatory requirement were made. Each resulting in a grade below the needed 70%. The managers at his new employer, Combined Insurance, were becoming less than optimistic with his chances of success within their sales organization. No one knew at the time, he suffered from dyslexia. Even though he knew the material, written exams were not the best way to assess his knowledge.

Persistence was rewarded not only with a passing grade but also an exclusive geographic territory to saturate with accident insurance policies. The territory was demographically sparse (translation: it was in a very rural community with very little population) The kind of area where a necktie-clad salesman driving a 1976 puke-pink thunderbird with a deer-damaged front was not the most welcomed by the local citizens. It was the kind of place that meaningless addresses required reliance on directions based on crumbling barns past such and such creek.

Instead of complaining about the quality of the assignment, he embraced it. He felt he had a natural connection with the area's inhabitants. He knew that he could not only survive, he could thrive. He had to. There were bills to pay and two hungry boys at home chirping "feed me, feed me."

He managed to exceed all expectations and eventually set national sales records that still exist to this day.

During the Combined Insurance era, he met one of the greatest influences in his professional career, W. Clement Stone. The leadership and common sense ideas learned would remain with him during his entire insurance career.

As a pre-teen, I remember attending award ceremonies and carrying boxes of awards, plaques and trophies that my father received. My brother and I couldn't help but notice: Our dad was kind of a big deal. We were taking nicer vacations, the family vehicles were upgraded and there was a noticeable increase in the amount and quality of the gifts under the Christmas tree. Life in the Hill family was good.

Fast forward to 1986. I was no longer a teenager. I had dropped out of college to chase the dream of rock stardom. I had become quite proficient at playing the role of starving musician and relegating myself to becoming a vagabond on the road as a light engineer for an up-and-coming country singer named Reba McEntire. My father had changed companies a few years prior to a little-known company called American Family Life Assurance Company and continued his successful run.

After crashing for an extended period at my parent's house (who were now living in Lubbock, Texas due to promotions) during a hiatus from the road, I finally was convinced to cut my hair, upgrade my wardrobe and give the insurance business a chance by the "Master Recruiter" himself – Jimmy Hill.

The Hill Family portrait. Circa 1986.

The decision seemed like a no-brainer. My father was the State Manager of the organization. My brother had followed in Dad's footsteps and was making a name for himself in the insurance business as well. I had seen the awards with their names on them piling up. If they could do it, my success was guaranteed! (Remember: I was not far removed from the overconfident teenage years.)

My plan was simple. Just check these boxes: 1. Pass the exam, 2. Go to the obligatory sales school, 3. Watch my dad make a sale and repeat his sales pitch verbatim to some folks (guaranteed to close every sale) and 4. buy that red Ferrari 308 GTS that I had so desired. Easy.

Unfortunately, it wasn't quite so easy after all. Boxes 1 and 2 were easily checked, but it was parts 3 and 4 that posed the problem.

Remember that little part about my father stuttering? His technique was…..unique. The presentation that I witnessed bore no resemblance to the one that was shown in the sales school. I had diligently committed it to memory. Not by a longshot. I was completely confused and embarrassed by his pitch. All of I could think of was how we could slink away with our dignity intact. My teenage assessment of my dad was now undeniably proven to be correct. And I needed a new mentor if I was going to afford my Ferrari!

Then, a bizarre thing happened, something that completely defied all the logic that I had managed to accrue in my 20 years on this earth. The lady that seemed to patiently endure the so-called "presentation" said,

"This sounds great. How do I sign up?" What? How could she possibly say yes? I was stunned.

Flushed with success, my father suddenly developed a confident strut as we walked across the parking lot.

"Your old man has still got it! What'd you think about that?!? Hope you paid close attention…"

I was completely at a loss for words. What had just happened? More importantly, (in my recently teenage mind) how in the world can I replicate what I had just seen? Had I made a huge mistake? The dream of Ferrari ownership was rapidly fading.

This was my first real lesson - People naturally buy from people that they can connect with. People that they can trust. If his "pitch" had been too slick, it would have missed the mark. His presentation was perfect in its imperfection. I was too "smart" to actually realize it at the time.

Over the years, my father, brother and I shared many sales adventures – from boardroom meetings with Fortune 500 CEOs to offering cancer insurance policies to parking lot attendants to handing out fudge samples at the Regency Square Mall in Richmond. There was always a common thread though – people are people. Treat them with the respect that they deserve. Truly care for them and place their needs above yours and success will find you.

Greg, Jimmy and Jay Hill. 1988

A Long, Successful Career

There is a relatively small plaque somewhat hidden in the lobby of the tower at Aflac Worldwide Headquarters. Countless people have passed it without even giving it a glance. This plaque is inscribed with a few names of folks that came from a different era. Most of them, unfortunately, have become footnotes in the company's history - relegated to a forgotten past. Time moves on.

If you are not familiar with Aflac beyond recognizing the duck, the company was started way back in 1955 largely through the efforts of a man by the name of John Amos and his brothers. There is a book chronicling the company's early history called "The Man from Enterprise" and I highly recommend it.

Jimmy with John and Elena Amos, 1987

Aflac has grown to become a dominant force in the insurance industry throughout the years while becoming a household name. This success was reached through the efforts of many dedicated individuals who suffered through personal financial difficulties, high levels of rejection and countless hours away from their families.

There are a select few folks that had the largest impact on the company's growth. These individuals are the groundbreakers. They set the foundation for the rewards many reap today. The lessons and wisdom that these mentors impart should not only be heeded but be applied each and every day. Savvy members of the current sales force should not only respect, but thank these folks for the sacrifices that were endured.

These trailblazers have been honored with

induction into Aflac's Hall of Fame. It is their names that are inscribed on the plaque.

My father, Jimmy Hill, is one of those names. He is a legend.

Jimmy Hill, Aflac Hall of Fame, Columbus, GA

I consider myself fortunate that I was able to be a part of his journey along with my mother and brother. Over the years, he would attempt to impart his wisdom to his *somewhat* receptive progenies. Throughout the organization, he became known for delivering commonsense sayings based on his observations and experiences. We affectionately labeled them "Jimmyisms" and they usually made their appearance during motivational speeches in front of the organization or meetings with his managers. This earned him the nickname of "The Reverend".

He never relied on a script during these speeches. He preferred to free-style. Sometimes, he would have a scrap of paper with bullet points, however, these could only be deciphered by him (I think…). I'm not sure if he even referred to them during the heat of the moment.

The audience members were always treated to a tremendous display of enthusiasm. On more than one occasion, I overheard folks exclaiming "I am excited! I don't know what I'm excited about, but I'm sooo excited!!".

The actual Jimmyisms tended to be a bit confusing leading to many befuddled looks. What usually soon followed was either myself or my brother being approached for clarification. We were essentially viewed as his interpreters. Unfortunately, neither of us were fluent in "Jimmyese!"

When all is said and done, the real legacy a parent can leave with a child is wisdom. My father chose to leave his legacy by setting a great example of leadership based on giving to others. He has positively affected countless lives throughout his amazing career helping others achieve personal and professional goals while living out their dreams.

As the years have rapidly flown past, I have enjoyed sharing my own bits of wisdom based on personal experiences and observations. I've conducted countless sales training sessions and seminars in front of thousands of eager salespeople in addition to mentoring motivated entrepreneurs. As I reach the twilight years of my own career, I find myself analyzing and referring to the "Jimmyisms" during my sessions. I have become a master at speaking and understanding "Jimmyese!"

My father has had a life-long dream to write a book entitled "Even D Students Can Make It Too". I think the non-fulfillment of this dream has been one of his regrets. This book is a tribute to him.

It contains most of the Jimmyisms that we can recall. I've tried to make it simple by categorizing the Jimmyisms, attempting to define them while sharing a story or two or three. Simple, *re*memorable (another Jimmy term) and usable - just as he would like it to be.

A bit of a disclaimer, though. Dad was a voracious reader. He would spend months slowly reading and digesting a book. "The Magic of Thinking Big", "Think and Grow Rich", "The Greatest Salesman in the World" – these are some of his Sales Bibles. I am not sure if some of the Jimmyisms come as a result or were taken by him from any of the books that he has so cherished. I mean no disrespect to any of the original authors of these quotes or in anyway intend to slight their creative ideas or concepts. Whatever their source of origin, my dad has truly believed in them, embraced them and lived them.

Of all the lessons that I have learned over the years, one that I can without a doubt confirm is very true: The older I get, the smarter my dad becomes...

Hopefully, my kids will say the same thing one day.

II

"Every Day is a Holiday and Every Meal is a Feast"

It's all about your Attitude and Perception

We are all given fantastic opportunities each and every day. Whether we choose to perceive them positively or negatively is completely up to us. Is the day going to be a holiday or is it going to be yet another miserable day? Is the meal going to be a fabulous feast suitable for royalty or is it simply going to serve as a means to stave off hunger pangs?

The choice is yours.

"They say it's the best!"

Whether it was a hot dog from a convenience store outside of Dillwyn, Virginia or table saw on sale at Sears Roebuck, the pure enthusiasm displayed by my father for his favorite things has always amazed me. We've lost count of the times that he would implore us to make a quick detour because "you have to try the barbeque at such and such place. they say it's the best!"

We've never really figured out who "they" are and we're not really sure what credentials "they" possess in order to make these proclamations, but dad has definitely been their voice and cheerleader. We have always made the detour based on the recommendation.

In sales, people can feel your passion. Your true belief in the product or service that you are providing. The attitude of "*You have to believe in it to sell it*" (yet another Jimmyism) is paramount to your longevity in sales. If you don't, find something that you do believe in. If you feel that the company that you represent is not the best, make a change and go to the best.

Who "*They*" are is really "*you*" and your opinion.

"Never worked, never will"

"Jimmy Hill, never worked and never will". If you meet him for the first time, this is usually how he introduces himself. He fervently believes that if you truly enjoy your career, then you aren't really having to work. If you are impassioned with your job, then you really aren't working.

It's Monday morning. The alarm clock rings. You have a choice: *You can roll over and go back to sleep, or roll out of bed and go to work.* We have all faced this crossroad at some time or another in our lives. Do we really enjoy being in our chosen career? Are we genuinely excited about going to "work"? Do we feel like we are making a difference or are we simply putting in time to get a paycheck? Did we make the right choice?

It all revolves around attitude. We continually see it in our daily lives. The checkout clerk that is really *checked out.* We complain about the lack of service that we receive from the waiter at the restaurant. We fume about being placed on hold when connecting with a dispassionate call center employee.

But then there are those moments. The time that you *just know* the person that you are interacting with truly loves their career. You can feel their passion. To them, it's not just a job.

The odds are extremely high that they chose to joyfully *roll out of bed* and get moving because they have found their calling. They never work….and never will. Because to them, it isn't work if you love what you do.

This leads to a simple question of self-introspection. Ask yourself: do you "work" or not?

"If You're Waiting on Me, You're Backing Up"

No one has ever been able to accuse Jimmy of being a procrastinator. In fact, he has lived a life exactly the opposite. We're all constantly inundated with motivational quotes such as Thomas Jefferson's "Never put off for tomorrow, what you can do today" or "Procrastination is the bad habit of putting off until the day after tomorrow what should have been done the day before yesterday." from Napoleon Hill (no relation!). They sound great, but do you truly practice them?

The very first payroll account that I was assigned

when I began my sales career was the El Paso School System in Texas. My job was to present cancer insurance policies to employees of the school system and assist in enrolling any interested folks. Newer agents like myself were typically paired up with a veteran agents which gave us an opportunity to learn the ropes. We would then go from school to school, set up shop in a teacher's lounge and sell, sell, sell.

By luck of the draw, I was paired up with a veteran agent, Johnny Gonzalez. Even though he was only a couple of years older than me, Johnny was one of the top performing agents in the organization. Due to his veteran status, it was assumed that he would present to and enroll any teachers as they came into the lounge. If another teacher arrived during his presentation, it was up to me to present and enroll. Truthfully, I vividly remember constantly glancing at the door, willing it to *not* open while Johnny made sale after sale. I was petrified of having to give a presentation (plus, we were splitting commissions. I was making money without having to do anything!).

I was perfectly fine with just waiting. Maybe I could attempt a presentation the next day....or the next. Whenever. I'd get around to it sometime.

Finally, the time came for me to finally give a presentation. Actually, I was forced to.

As Johnnie was deep into a presentation to one of the teachers, he looked over at me and instructed, "Can you go to the cafeteria and pick up some applications? I presented to the workers down there yesterday and some of them wanted to talk it over with their spouses."

Realizing that this should be a simple task, I rushed out the door (before it suddenly opened and then I would have to actually present to a teacher!) and headed to the cafeteria. Once there, I found the supervisor and inquired about the applications. She seemed a bit confused, but directed the staff to take seats and listen to my pitch.

I was completely confused! I was only there to pick up applications….not to make a dreaded presentation! At this point, I nervously gave what I would honestly describe as one of the top ten worst presentations in the history of sales. My hands shook so much that the brochure that I clung to began to flap - completely distracting the audience. The more I tried to calm down the worse it got. I just wanted to get out of this situation and look for a new career.

Then, a bizarre thing happened. The cafeteria workers actually began to fill out the applications. Despite my horrible presentation, they actually wanted my product. Maybe I didn't suck as bad as I thought I did!

Flush with success, I strutted back to the teacher's lounge. I could not wait to report my results to Johnny. I could not wait for my old man to hear that his son was a chip off the old block. I was stoked! Hmm..Maybe that Ferrari was still in play afterall.

Upon relaying the information to Johnny, he was excited as well. Except for one minor detail: Whether he had misspoke or I misunderstood, the meeting was actually supposed to be with the *custodial* workers. The meeting for the cafeteria workers was scheduled for the next day!

During the rest of the enrollment, I found myself wanting to be the presenter. My confidence had grown because I simply did it. I no longer wanted to *wait*...I wanted to *do*.

Years later, I attended the Rapport Leadership Institute in Nevada. The final requirement for graduation was a test to see if you could conquer the fear of public speaking in a less-than-conducive environment. We were all instructed to dress in professional attire and were then driven to a pre-determined location – a parking lot of a car wash center in the heart of Las Vegas...on a busy, sunny Sunday afternoon. At this point, we lined up and informed that we were to recite the pledge of allegiance at the top of our lungs. This recitation must be at such a volume that our teacher could hear it all the way across this noisy parking lot.

As bemused bystanders watched my classmates fail in succession, I became anxious. Just as I had felt years before in the El Paso High School cafeteria, I just wanted to leave. Maybe we could do this later, when there weren't as many onlookers. Maybe it would be a bit quieter.

There was no backing out now. I could not put off taking this final exam. It was my turn.

Interestingly enough, the moment I began to recite the pledge, the world around me disappeared and I felt truly focused. The smirking crowd of car wash clients that were receiving free entertainment became meaningless. I must succeed. There was pure jubilation as I was given the thumbs up – I had passed.

What is the lesson learned from this? *The waiting is the hardest part.* (shout out to Tom Petty). It is easy to procrastinate. When faced with a task, instead of putting things off, your attitude should be "If you're waiting on me, your backing up!"

Which leads us to…

"I don't want mine in the sweet by and by, I want mine in the sweet now and now"

By human nature, we tend to come up with every possible excuse to put off today what we can probably do tomorrow or the next day. We suffer from the old "paralysis of analysis" instead of just jumping in and actually *doing* the task.

Time has a way of slipping past. How many times have you regretted not doing something in life? Or waited too long and the opportunity passes by without action on your part.

Would've. Could've. Should've.

"Does a Cat Have a Climbing Gear?"

This simply translates to my dad's way of answering in the affirmative: an enthusiastic "Yes!" However, upon further analysis, we have come to the conclusion that it also contains a bit of a hidden meaning. One that deals with an extreme level of motivation.

Like many families, we had dogs and cats as pets while growing up. Two of these feline family members went by the names of "Willie" and "Scat Cat". Dad had adopted them from the owners of a cabinet shop in Farmville, Virginia. You probably guessed it, the cabinet shop was a client of his and he had provided their employees with the opportunity to participate in valuable insurance programs.

Dad was fascinated with Willie and Scat Cat. He actually studied their 'sales techniques.' He loved to boast of Willie's alpha-male leadership skills. The consistent display of reserved confidence and the smooth strut. He was constantly amused at Scat Cat's ability to then trump Willie's attempt at maintaining even the slightest amount of dominance in the relationship.

The cats accompanied our family as we moved across the country with each of Dad's promotions. Boise, Idaho to Lubbock, Texas, to Los Angeles, California and finally back home to Virginia. Willie and Scat Cat were always there. They lived (very) long lives.

During a manager's meeting in the late nineties, one of the regional managers was singled out by Jimmy and admonished for what he perceived as unacceptable performance results.

"You know...I could put my 21-year-old alley cat into your role, and she would do a better job than you! At least she wouldn't screw it up!" he chided. "You've got to step it up or we may have to find a different opportunity that better fits your motivation levels...."

The manager was indeed properly motivated and his team preceded to hit all sales goals which eventually earned him a promotion in the company. He still jokes to this day about the conversation and how it achieved the desired result.

"That was a happy day for me when I found out that damn cat died. I knew then at least one of my potential replacements was gone!", he has often said.

Cats, and humans, can accomplish great things when properly motivated. When chased by an aggressive dog, a cat can fly up a tree at an amazing pace. They do indeed have a "climbing gear."

Sometimes, we should find our own climbing gears in order to achieve greater success. It shouldn't require a rabid animal chasing us across the lawn to make us recognize this, although sometimes a little push doesn't hurt.

"He's got the Losers Limp"

Nearing the end of a ball game, have you ever noticed how many injuries suddenly occur from players on the team that looks like they have no hope of winning? They seem to give up all hope and begin to look for any and every excuse in order to justify their impending defeat. Around our household, this affliction was known as the "Loser's Limp".

While some injuries may actually be legitimate, it was amazing how a miracle healing soon takes place after the game. If one of us developed the Loser's Limp, we were usually called out on it and encouraged to fess up.

One of our cousins was particularly susceptible to

developing cases of Loser's Limp. He possessed fantastic athletic skills and eventually became a college athlete. Unfortunately, if a game was not headed in the right direction, his confident athletic stroll would suddenly turn into a noticeable limp. His attitude would become combative. Blame would be placed on everything from the opposing player to the condition of the field. Never on himself. When he finally learned the importance of controlling his emotions and refusing to make excuses, the loser's limp became less and less prevalent. Success on the field soon followed.

"1% is better than 0%"

If there is at least a tiny percent of a chance for success, that means that there still is a chance. You may remember the scene from Dumb and Dumber when Jim Carrey's character was given odds of one in a million. A smile came across as he digested this information. "So you're telling me there's a chance...yeah!".

In 1999, my dad faced similar odds when a traumatic accident threatened the loss of one of his eyes.

It was late summer on a typical Saturday evening. We were building a small stage for an event that my band would be performing at the next weekend. His workshop was stocked with every imaginable tool and he prided himself on his woodworking skills. He loved projects and completing them to perfection.

Given his many years of construction and building

experience, he was very proficient at using a nail gun. So confident in his mastery of this tool, he often shunned the use of any protective gear, including safety goggles.

Nearing completion, the rat-a-tat-tat of the nail gun could be heard as the stage took shape. Suddenly, it stopped as he shouted out.

"Oh lord, I've done done it now! I've shot my eye out!!"

A nail had gone directly into one of his eyes. He then preceded to pull the nail from his eye and summoned me over to examine it.

It was gruesome.

Luckily, we had the cell number of an eye surgeon that had just performed Lasik surgery on myself, my brother and my mother. Being that it was a Saturday, the doctor instructed us to meet him at his office immediately. (In a strange twist of fate, this doctor, Shawn Hobbs, has since become my neighbor and a great friend. We have lived next door to each other for the last 15 years).

For the first few days after the accident, all seemed to be fine and the eye seemed to be somewhat okay. On the fourth day, however, the recovery took a bad turn and we went into panic mode. Dr. Hobbs referred him to the Virginia Eye and Ear center in downtown Richmond. Upon examination, the doctor immediately called for emergency surgery. The prognosis was bleak.

My mother quizzed the doctor, "What do you mean? What are the odds of him losing his eyesight?"

"Ma'am, we not talking about losing his eyesight. I'm giving him about a 1% chance of saving his eye".

Without missing a beat, my father – solidifying

himself as the most optimistic person in the world – exclaimed:

"Well, there you go. The doctor just said that he is going to save my eye!".

"Jimmy", replied my mother. "He just said there is only a 1% chance of saving your eye. They are probably going to have to remove it".

"He said there is a 1% chance. That is way better than 0%. I'll take those odds. My eye will be just fine…".

True to his prediction. Not only was his eye saved, but his eyesight was saved as well.

As long as there is a chance - however slight it may be - you have to believe in success. You have to finish.

There were many times during our careers that it looked like meeting our annual quota was impossible. He never lost faith. He always remained optimistic that it was never over until the last application showed up on the production report. In fact, one year the annual quota of over $20 million in sales was exceeded by a mere $300 – the approximate cost of one policy.

Until all has ended, there still will be a chance.

"Don't let anybody steal your dream"

During the days with Combined Insurance, sales blitz events called "Ardmores" were commonplace. Ardmores typically required the organizations salespeople to travel to a specific town and stay in the same hotel. After attending a motivational morning meeting, the fired-up salespeople would aggressively market or "blitz" the local area selling accident insurance policies to any and everybody. "One, Two, Three, Four – Let's go door to door!" could frequently be heard throughout the hotel (actually motel) parking lot.

One of these events took place in the thriving metropolis of Lynchburg, VA. sometime in the mid-1970s. As kids, we were allowed to tag along which we viewed as an awesome vacation. They were great fun for us since we could go shopping, hang out at the pool or goof around while Dad was off selling and making some money.

As the story goes, there were a few sales reps hanging out in the parking lot immediately following the company-sponsored motivational morning meeting. They were conducting what we have come to refer to as a "trunk meeting". These meetings are in no way, shape or form considered motivational. The level of negativity at this particular one was particularly high.

"Jimmy, come over here", one of them called out.

Flushed with excitement from the rah-rah experience that he had just taken part in, he felt this would be a fantastic moment to glean nuggets of wisdom from experienced veterans. He quickly headed over.

Instead, he was greeted with comments such as: "Man, this place is the worst". "This is a waste of time, nobody here buys insurance". "It's supposed to rain. Cold-calling in weather like that just sucks...".

Completely demoralized, he reluctantly headed out to go "door to door, store to store 'til there ain't no more". As his teammates had correctly predicted, no sales were to be made. Then, it began to rain. They were correct.

Realizing a bad streak was getting even worse, he headed to lunch at a local diner. All of the tables were full, so he took a spot at a barstool next to some guys that were obviously blue collar workers. Always ready to strike up a conversation, he asked the gentleman seated next to him what kind of business he was in. It just so happened they were construction workers and he was the boss/owner of their small company.

Given our family's history in construction, the two immediately hit it off. It seems that due to the rain, construction at the jobsite had come to a halt and they were killing time. Upon learning that Jimmy was selling accident insurance, the owner requested policies for all of his workers.

"Just stop by and sign 'em up at the end of the week", he said.

He quickly agreed while writing down the address of the construction site. In his mind, he had already made his weekly sales quota! Any other policies written during the rest of the week were just icing on the cake at this point. His attitude had completely changed. In fact, he was so motivated that he broke a sales record that week.

Unfortunately, either due to his writing down the wrong address of the construction site or poor navigational skills, he never found the contractor on that Friday!

He has always credited this chance meeting with a contractor in a diner that he never sold as completely changing his attitude and saving his career. Had he listened and believed the advice given by the teammates during the "trunk meeting", he probably would have never stayed in insurance sales. He did not allow them to steal his dream.

"A Goal is a Dream with a Deadline"

Blame it on bad luck. Call it bizarre twists of fate. They say that lightning doesn't strike twice. For Jimmy Hill, it has struck three times. Each of which has resulted in either his home or business being burned to the ground.

The first occurrence happened while he was in High School as he watched his boyhood home disintegrate. The second time, his beloved service station was eradicated due to a direct strike. The third time came in 1979.

A few years earlier, after moving to Virginia, Jimmy built his dream house on the "ridge" near Enonville with amazing views of the famous Blue Ridge Mountains. When I say "built", I literally mean "built". At the time he was a contractor and my grandfather owned the construction company. He took full advantage of the tools and equipment that were available to him along with contractor discounts on supplies.

He has always firmly believed that *"If you're gonna do something – do it right and do it with class"*. In keeping with this belief, he built a massive dwelling with over 6,000 square feet. Bear in mind, he had just lost his entire business to a fire only a few months before!

During the summer months in the 1970s, our family spent many weeks at our grandparent's place in Emerald Isle, NC enjoying beach activities. We were there in 1979 when we received a call late at night. Our house was struck by lightning and burned to the ground. We were in shock.

After a long, late night drive, we arrived at our still smoldering home. Or more appropriately: "former home". We had lost everything. I still vividly remember my mother's reaction of disbelief followed by a flowing of tears.

The Hill Family House Fire. Enonville, VA 1979

I remember my father's stoic acceptance of the catastrophe. I also remember his exact words only moments later:

"I will rebuild our house. I will have a roof over our heads by Christmas." This would have to be achieved only 5 months.

He had shared his dream. He had set a goal. He had set a deadline.

True to his word, we opened our Christmas presents

under the roof of our rebuilt home. A house built during limited free time away from his new "real" job – selling insurance policies for a company called American Family Life Assurance Company or, as it's known today, Aflac.

Quite a way to start a legendary career.

How did he accomplish these feats? Because he firmly believed he could. If you have a positive outlook on life. If you can remain optimistic in spite of tremendous setbacks, nothing can stand in the way of you achieving your goals and dreams. Just remember to set a deadline.

When I began my career in sales, I dreamed of Ferrari ownership. I wanted to attain this goal before I reached the age of 40. In 2001, at the age of 36, I was finally able to purchase that red Ferrari 308 GTS! Dream and Goal Attained!

"You've gotta be in the right vehicle"

As a kid, it was always fun to visit my grandparents home. My grandmother was a certified pack-rat which gave their house a bit of a disorganized museum feel. For us grandchildren, the exploration possibilities were plentiful. The discoveries were endless.

In my father's old room, numerous trophies filled the dressers as a testimony to his drag racing prowess. Adorned with golden race cars, we would hoist them in the air pretending to celebrate fictitious victories of our own. Oddly, dad always seemed a bit embarrassed by them and would only share the actual stories when we pushed him to. We were always mesmerized. According the legend, he held the standing quarter mile record for drag racing for a short period.

Racing has always played a big part in his life and our family weekends in the early 70's usually included heading out to a Nascar race and spending the day somewhere in the infield watching some of the best drivers of the time battle for a visit to victory lane. My grandfather's construction company was even a proud sponsor of Cecil Gordon's #24 and my dad became fast friends with many of the drivers.

One of these drivers happened to be the most successful driver in the history of autosport – Richard Petty. The King.

Their lifelong friendship began in the late 60's. Our neighbor on Waddell Street in Louisburg was employed by the King as his head of public relations and it was not long before an introduction was made. The two immediately hit it off. Our families spent many hours together at the Petty home and at post-race dinners. My brother and I fondly remember spirited games of Nerf football with the other kids while my mother enjoyed spending time in one of the vans with racer's wives including Lynda Petty.

Richard Petty and Jimmy. Circa 1990

In addition to being a "deadhead" in the Petty pit crew, my dad was also employed to cart Richard's "Million Dollar" winning race car to Winston Cup events and display it for adoring fans to enjoy. You can only imagine how much fun it was as a kid to play "race car driver" in the actual race car of the most famous driver on the planet!

Years later, we would become business partners with Ward Burton and his father, John. Dad had played a large part in introducing the Burtons to the Nascar elite of the day helping them get their feet in the door during a highly competitive era. Ward would eventually win the Daytona 500.

Naturally, a lot of the Jimmyisms reference racing in some form or another. Probably the most memorable of these used an analogy between the physical car with the company or brand that you represent. It goes something like this:

You can be the best driver in the world, however, if you are driving a VW bug against the fastest Nascar vehicles – winning becomes difficult if not impossible. You can be the greatest salesperson in the world, however, making sales becomes exponentially more challenging if the company that you represent or the product (or service) that you are touting is not competitive or subpar.

Additionally, the vehicle that you are driving today, or the company that you are representing now, may not be the best or fastest tomorrow. The most successful salespeople realize that in order to stay on top, they must continue to evolve and be willing to make a change if needed. If they enjoy being in victory lane on a continuous basis, they will proactively search for and represent the best.

Richard Petty holds the world record for most victories in racing history – 200. A record that will probably never be broken. Many pundits over the years have pointed to the vehicles that he had access to and raced to victory (along with having a stellar pit crew) gave him an unfair advantage. We all know the cliché "Life is not always fair." Throughout history, winners have always recognized and utilized every advantage currently available – but they are also constantly on the outlook for the next best, fastest vehicle.

In keeping with the racing theme, this leads us to another Jimmyism:

"The Bicycle is the Fastest Vehicle on Earth"

Why? *" Nobody has ever been able to crank one up all the way!" - Jimmy Hill*

"Enjoy the Miserable Time I'm Having"

From the viewpoint of us kids, our family vacations were awesome. Summer trips were usually spent in Emerald Isle, North Carolina. Our daytime hours were filled with playing on the beach, jumping waves and lounging on beach chairs. The evening hours consisted of dinner at one of our favorite seafood restaurants such as Sanitary Fish Market in Morehead City or Cap't Charlies in Swansboro followed by an exciting round of putt-putt, a spirited go-kart race or a bike ride. Our parent's viewpoint was quite different.

Money and finances were constantly on their minds. It frustrated my father that we couldn't afford beachfront accommodations. He was embarrassed that we had to carry our chairs across a busy highway while avoiding "rock, busted glass and cuckleberries."

Years later, he would joke that my brother and I had obviously learned to read restaurant menus from the right to left, always choosing the most expensive item as he winced.

"Hungry Birds" ordering from the right side of the menu. 1960's

My parents never let on to us at the time that money was an issue. They were more concerned that our childhoods would be filled with a carefree happiness.

Dad had finally tired of 'enjoying the miserable time he was having' on vacation and decided there had to be a change. He made a conscious decision that things must change. We would enjoy beachfront accommodations in the future. The price of a meal would no longer determine the choice of our restaurant. We would even order desserts without a guilty conscience! This was his dream. (Along with motorhome ownership which he purchased several.)

The dream was believable. It was achievable.

"Stinkin' Thinkin'"

As much as we would like to believe that

maintaining a positive mental outlook will always result in positive outcomes in each and every endeavor, unfortunately, it is not realistic. There will be days when nothing seems to go as planned. You try to remain optimistic but negative thoughts eventually creep in and the spiral of pessimism commences.

You hope that things will change for the better, however, they just seem to be getting worse. Cries of "you have gotta be kidding me!" suddenly escape your mouth. You've got a case of *Stinkin' Thinkin'*.

Dad's cure for stinkin' thinkin' was quite simple and will probably sound a bit silly, but it actually works.

"Stop what you are doing immediately. You're just making it worse. Go to the rest room and tear off a piece of toilet paper. Get a pen and write your negative thoughts on that piece of toilet paper and flush them down the commode."

On more than a few occasions, I've had to almost use up an entire roll!

Common sense tells us that there is no way that flushing a piece of toilet paper down a commode could possibly change our fortunes. If that were true, I would highly advice the purchase of stock in every paper company!

It is the psychology behind the ability to *physically* do something to reduce your level of frustration. Instead of doing something that you will later regret such as punching a wall, this simple, symbolic act may be the needed antidote for *Stinkin' Thinkin'*.

III

"Follow the Person, Not the Title"

Thoughts on Leadership, Management and Team Building

Throughout time, there have those who seek to quantify and categorize specific characteristics required for success in a given field. They study and rank the necessary ingredients in an attempt to create a template for perfection. Tests and assessments have been developed and carefully scrutinized in order to develop odds for candidate ascendancy. High level corporate director appointment decisions are often based on these investigative recommendations.

I'm pretty sure that there have been blueprints developed which list the fundamental components needed to identify the perfect candidate for leadership positions. I would also guess that an analyst would be not be inclined to check many of the boxes on this list when examining Jimmy Hill for leadership potential.

He was a poor student in school with lackluster grades. He had a speech impediment and was difficult to understand. Communicating his thoughts and ideas are frequently met with confused expressions. Fortunately, he does possess many of the qualities that cannot be quantified by algorithms displayed on an unemotional report.

Those that have had the privilege to serve under his tutelage would concur - Jimmy Hill is the very embodiment of a leader. He should be the model. This model, unfortunately, is not duplicatable.

We can, however, heed real-world recommendations and sage advice.

My father has always been vocal about the quality of the leadership above him - good or bad. He has studied and mimicked those that he respected while openly criticizing those that he has deemed to be simply masquerading as leaders. *"Going to a class on leadership, doesn't make you a leader. You can learn some concepts and maybe pick up a few good ideas, however, you have to live your life as a leader. Your people's issues and difficulties should become yours. You have to completely be bought-in and 'walk the walk'."*

"You Gotta Clean the Dishes Before You Can Make the Meal"

At the stroke of midnight on January 1st, 1987, a moving truck containing the belongings of the Hill family from Buckingham, Virginia - the county that recently had its first stoplight installed - pulled up at a house in Rancho Palos Verdes, California - a suburb of the Los Angeles metropolis. Close behind, a cassette player in a 1985 Ford Taurus could be heard playing the tune "Country Boy, You've Got Your Feet in LA" by Glen Campbell. Jimmy Hill and his family had made their entrance and were ready to embark on a new, exciting journey - one that would eventually change their lives along with many others. Eventually, this arrival would bring numerous marketing opportunities along with the development of ground-breaking strategies for American Family Life and its field force. Benefits that are still reaped to this day. The second gold rush was on!

Historically, the California market had proven to be a difficult one for American Family Life to crack by the late 1980's. Lackluster sales had contributed to a constant turnover of sales management along with a completely disorganized field sales force.

The Jimmy Hill era did not start well.

Imagine this: You move your family to one of the most expensive areas in the country. Your income is based on the sales performance of your organization.

And....your first week's sales report comes in with a big, fat $0 in production. Absolutely no insurance business had been during the previous week. None. Welcome to LA.

A few weeks passed with similar results. It was now time for the much anticipated kick-off meeting in which the proud sales professionals of the Southern California/Los Angeles State Organization would finally be introduced to their new leader. Home office guests that had flown across the country from Columbus, Georgia were in attendance. The meeting room was decorated with motivational quotes and posters encouraging sales folks to "Qualify for the 1987 National Convention in the tropical paradise of Hawaii". A smorgasbord of food was readied for the enjoyment of the attendees. The excitement level was....well..... non-existent.

In fact, I recall having a conversation with one of the attendees in the hallway as he pitched the advantages and amazing opportunities associated with a life insurance company that he worked with. Apparently, he had not been apprised to the relationship that I had with his new manager.

Realizing the atmosphere was not to his liking, Jimmy addressed the crowd with one of the more interesting motivational speeches that I have ever witnessed. It went something like this:

"Hi. I'm Jimmy Hill - your new State Manager. I want to make a few things perfectly clear from the very beginning. Number One: In your invitation to this function, I requested that you bring some new policy applications along so that we could overnight them in to be processed. Two of you folks did. Johnnie and Parviz. Come on up here. I'd like to personally thank you for bringing applications in and reward you with checks for $50.00 each. Number Two: You've heard there are no free lunches. Well, that applies today. I've asked the hotel to box up these lunches and give them to the homeless. Number Three: At this point, every person in this sales organization will be losing their appointments to represent American Family Life Assurance Company of Columbus, Georgia as of today. If you would like to discuss a future with this company, I will be glad to meet with you in my office at any time.

I heard some of you joking about the revolving door of managers that have occupied this role. You are probably thinking that you can wait and I'll be soon gone and you can just take advantage of the next guy. You are wrong. I did not move my family across this country to fail. Get a good look at this face - Jimmy Hill is going no where. We WILL succeed here. Meeting Adjourned." The audience was stunned.

Jimmy soon received a phone call. The founder of the company and CEO, John Amos and the President, Dan Amos were on the line.

"Uh, Jimmy," Dan said. "Did I just hear right? Did you just fire the entire sales team out there?"

"Yes", he replied. "Yes I did. There was no sales team here. I'm going to start this thing from scratch and build it the way it should have been built in the first place. I just washed the dishes. Now I can cook the meal."

Dan responded, "Well, I expect you're right. You have our full support. You do what you need to do!"

The rest made Aflac history.

As a result of his tenacity, along with his later business partner and co-state manager, Bill Krzciok (AKA: Kry-Zookie), the California organization became the fastest growing market in the company and continues to be one of the most vital components for its overall sales.

Jimmy, Greg and Bill Krzciok. Circa 1988. California.

New strategies such as utilizing Section 125 of the IRS tax code to benefit clients and drive new sales opportunities were developed. The City and County of Los Angeles were obtained as accounts due to utilizing the new approach of establishing broker relationships.

During his induction into the Aflac Hall of Fame, Dan Amos credited Jimmy and the Southern California team with "bringing Broker to Aflac."

It all started with "cleaning the dishes."

(Some factual notes: we actually did arrive at our house at midnight on New Year's Eve in 1987. This early arrival became a running joke with our next door neighbors, the Brunstroms, for many years. They applauded the full maximization of our rental contract. And, yes, we were listening to Glen Campbell. He has been one of Dad's absolute favorite artists and he felt the

song was a perfect fit for the occasion. Additionally, he actually did put the entire field sales force on notice – many of whom came back to Aflac!)

"Success is Not Always Convenient"

Over the years, advancements in technology has made life easier. I can still remember the excitement using of our first copying machine. The word processor replacing our typewriter which was then replaced with the computer. Paper applications replaced by laptop programs which eliminated the need for "overnighting" business via Fedex in order to meet a sales quota. Greater levels of efficiency equate into more productivity time.

My dad was quite proud of the fact that he was the first manager in Aflac to not only receive a company paid cellular phone but also to secure the first fax machine. He has always been a supporter of the advantages of using technology, however, allowing it to distract from the fundamentals of salesmanship was frowned upon. One of his pet peeves has been entering an office and hearing people "tap, tap, tap" on a computer keyboard instead of engaging in conversation.

On multiple occasions, I was reprimanded by him for 'taking the easy route' by attempting to solve an issue via email.

"Get your butt in the car and go see them face-to-face. It may be inconvenient, but it's the right thing to do. Don't take the easy way out. That way there will be no confusion. Plus, they will see you as the person who goes

above and beyond."

Assuming the role of leadership in an organization, one must be cognizant that people are paying close attention to the actions and activities of the leader. Jimmy has always prided himself that he would never ask anyone in the organization to do anything that he would not at least attempt himself.

"How can you tell someone to go sell an insurance policy when you've never sold one yourself? A leader leads by example.", he often said.

Success is not always convenient. Do what others are not willing to do. If it requires waking up at 3:30am in the morning in order to see a group of construction workers. Do it. If there is a late-night shift of workers that need assistance. Do it. Make the sacrifice. Success is for those that can and will be inconvenienced.

"Communication Will Always be the Key"

You are nervous about sending the email to your boss, but you know it's important. The situation has to be addressed. Your index finger hovers over the send button. You still debate yourself. Should I send it? How will it be received? Will my boss be disappointed in me when its read?

Click. It's sent.

Now for the even harder part. You wait for a response. The clock ticks. Nothing. No response. A few hours pass. Still nothing. Maybe it ended up in the spam folder. Maybe the boss is just locked out of their email account. The hours stretch into the next day. Paranoia begins to set in. What if your boss is upset by your email?

A few days pass and you suddenly go into full-on panic mode. What if the boss thinks that your email is so insignificant that it doesn't even merit a response? What if *you* are so insignificant in the eyes of your boss that you don't even warrant at least a quick reply of "got it. checking on it now. I'll get back to you ASAP" ? Then you become upset. You have lost respect and faith in your leader.

The best leaders are the best communicators. Unanswered emails and unreturned calls are noticed by the people in your organization. Not only is a lack of communication unprofessional, it is *"downright lazy."* Jimmy held the firm opinion that: ***"I don't care if you're the President of the United States, you ain't that busy to return a damn call! There are 24 hours in a day. Plenty of time to at least email somebody back. Don't leave them hanging!"***

A great example of a master communicator was one of my former bosses and friends, Ken Cofer.

Ken began his career with Aflac in the early 1970's in Virginia. Many considered him to be a bit gruff, however, I always enjoyed being around him. He and Jimmy became friends very early on and remained close

---

throughout the years.

(A good indicator that you had "made it" into my dad's inner circle was his designation of a nickname for you. Ken's assigned nickname was "the doctor".)

I'm 100% positive that the greatest day in Ken's life was the day that the cell phone was introduced for sale to the public. He lived on the phone. It did not matter where he was at the particular time, the cell phone would be answered and issue would be addressed.

It was a bit annoying, however, to be in the middle of your backswing during a round of golf and hear 'Hello, Ken Cofer, how can I help you?" in the background!

Ken firmly believed in the power of communication and practiced it on a consistent basis. As a member of his team, you knew that you could count on a quick response which created a feeling of reassurance.

I'm sure that my dad wholeheartedly approved.

"Panic Management Never Works"

Most businesses rely on new sales to drive their profitability. Business plans are developed focusing on strategies, tactics, indicators and metrics. A sales force is acquired, sales training programs are established and tweaked. Marketing initiatives are put in place. Management structures are developed and effectiveness levels are closely tracked.

When sales are up, all is well. Times are good. Budgets open up and everyone in the organization celebrates. Confidence permeates the culture.

When sales are down, heads are scratched and fingers are pointed around the management team. Blame is hurled in order to deflect from personal management or leadership shortcomings. Career security is jeopardized and position longevity is questioned. The organizational culture becomes toxic. An air of panic begins to set in.

The most alarming consequence of panic management is typically a noticeable shift in the style of leadership employed. Managers that until recently supported a culture of creativity and team input suddenly become *demanding dictators*. Rash decisions are made. Inexplicable changes are implemented. Unproven strategies are employed. Team members begin to feel undeserving and under-appreciated. The panic level increases and eventually the business or organization is doomed.

Historically, overall sales results tend to be cyclical. Every organization will have highs and lows. Much to their dismay, quota-busting sales teams are typically rewarded with increasingly difficult sales expectations for subsequent years.

Albert Einstein once famously said: "Compound interest is the eighth wonder of the world. It is the most powerful force in the universe."

Sales quotas and expectations are similar to compound interest. In order for a business to grow, quotas are and must be based on the previous year's results. They are not based on sales figures from 10 years ago.

In every company or organization, there seem to be wily veterans. The folks that seem to have been around forever. What's their secret? How have they 'survived' for so long?

A common trait that most seem to share is consistency. They remain calm through challenging times. While understanding the need to remain relevant in their chosen field of business, they implement changes methodically. If sales results suddenly take a downturn, instead of making drastic changes, they begin to make minor adjustments. These adjustments can slowly become major overhauls if needed. They understand and truly believe that the basic strategies and tactics employed previously have worked and should not be quickly abandoned.

The key is: they *do not* panic.

Let's compare a sales organization to driving a car.

The manager is typically in the driver's seat while the salespeople are passengers. The passengers usually have directional input or may be allowed to give driving advice (back seat drivers!), however, the driver is the one who ultimate steers the vehicle.

Have you ever ridden with a driver who makes 'jerky' motions when turning the steering wheel? It probably made you a bit nervous and uncomfortable.

If the driver, or manager, makes a sudden exaggerated turn - bad things usually happen. Passengers can be thrown around the car. Some may get sick. Some may be tossed outside. The vehicle may even crash!

The best drivers are smooth. They never oversteer when operating a vehicle. As a passenger, you hardly notice even the sharpest of curves. You are confident in their abilities and trust them explicitly. They have your life in their hands and you are okay with that. They live long, accident free lives because they resist the urge to panic in a crisis situation.

Aspire to be the best driver, or manager/leader. Don't panic and always remember your passengers are relying on you to get them to their destinations safely.

"Every Loser Knows a Winner"

Southern California. Sometime between 1987 and 1989. The sales organization had finally started to trend in a positive direction. The culture had developed into one of positivity. A call was received from the founder of the company, John Amos, congratulating the team for "being well ahead of sales expectations."

This turnaround was a direct result of the persistent new salesperson recruiting efforts of Jimmy and the management team. The key to growing a sales organization is and always will be a focus on a *"duplication of efforts."* Two people can do twice what one can do. Double those results with four people, etc.

My father has possessed a unique ability to strike up conversations with complete strangers throughout his life. His attitude toward 'cold-calling' potential clients is *"there's a friend that I haven't met yet standing on the other side of that door.* "

During one of his recruiting 'blitzes", Jimmy struck gold, but it didn't come to him easily, he had to dig DEEP to strike this vein.

While mom and dad were finalizing the lease on their new state office in the Los Angeles area, Jimmy struck up a friendly and personal conversation with their commercial real estate leasing agent, Peggy. She was a very sweet and hardworking lady that was smack in the middle of a divorce. She described the reason for her divorce as "the Amway business." Peggy went on to tell my father about how the business, and other things, took a major toll on her marriage. Peggy also mentioned that the whole Amway experience "ruined" her husband's once successful insurance career.

Jimmy and Margaret shared their Amway experience with Peggy and they, no doubt, consoled each other. However, after they got done with their brief Amway pity party, Jimmy informed Peggy that American Family was now hiring in L.A., and he gently asked Peggy if her husband "still had an active insurance license." Peggy shook her head, yes, but then went on to caution Jimmy about her husband's current outlook. She didn't paint the rosiest picture of Roy, indicating that he was "pretty beaten up." Undaunted, and digging in to find a winner, Jimmy asked for Roy's phone number. Within a week, Roy had an appointment to sell insurance with the company. As it turns out, Roy wasn't ready to go to work. Roy attended some training, but didn't sell a single policy...he didn't even make a single sales call.

Most sales managers would have wished Roy well and bid him adieu, but not James R. Hill. Of course, Jimmy was confident that "every loser knows a winner," and he was dead set to get Roy to lead him to one. In a casual phone conversation about the Amway experience and all of the nonsense (and non-success) that that business led to, Jimmy simply asked Roy, "who's the sharpest licensed insurance agent you know?" Roy thought for a moment and then replied, "A guy named, Joe. In fact, he was in Amway too."

During their days in Amway, Roy and Peggy had become acquainted with this budding entrepreneur who had rapidly risen to the Emerald level and had become a top draw on the company's motivational speaker circuit. However, this guy's career had met a similar fate to most and he resigned, pursuing other avenues. Roy then mentioned to Jimmy that this guy, Joe, had gone back into his previous trade. He was a life and health agent right there in L.A.

Jimmy handed the number over to Jay and he placed a call to this failed Amway wunderkind. Jay asked Joe if he'd drive down to the Torrance area to meet Jimmy. When Joe learned that Jimmy was buying lunch, he agreed and a few days later, this guy named, Joe, had a writing number with American Family. His full name was Joe Buzzello, but he was dubbed, "Gospel Joe" for reasons nobody remembers. Joe made an extremely positive impression on my father and brother. It appears that the feeling was mutual.

And then, as always, there's the REST of the story.

Joe's enthusiasm and creativity would play a major part in the extremely rapid growth that was witnessed by Aflac during the late 1980s into the 1990s and beyond. Not long after the Hill family returned to their Virginia roots and Co-State Manager Bill Krzciok (AKA-Kry-Zookie) ended his run in Southern California, Joe ascended to the role of State Sales Coordinator of Los Angeles, leading the organization to unprecedented heights. Through Joe's guidance, that legacy team soared to become one of the most consistently high-performing teams in the company. This eventually led to Joe's induction into Aflac's West Territory Hall of Fame.

Jimmy had, yet again, shook a man's hand, looked over his shoulder and found a winner. Every loveable loser knows one. You just have to ask them.

My father was arguably one of the most successful recruiters in the history of Aflac. The number of successful agents and managers counts in the hundreds if not thousands. He has always been proud of the fact that many of these folks went on to become leaders in not only Aflac, but other companies as well. At last count, 27 people that he either recruited or mentored went on to become state level managers in Aflac - the same position that he held for over 20 years. That is a legacy.

His recruiting philosophy was simple: "*You never know what someone is going through in their personal and professional lives."* If you are in a position to make a positive difference in their lives, do it. Don't stereotype them and prejudge their success potential. They just need that chance to prove it.

"Praise, Recognition and Appreciation"

What motivates a salesperson? Can you pick one specific thing?

As a young district manager, I was very proud of my team. We were motivated and aggressive. We usually resided at or near the top of the rankings in sales performance. I was also fortunate to have the top agent in the entire company on the team at the time, Alan Bradshaw.

Alan, or "Big Al", was a selling machine. A master at the art of sales, time management guru and genuinely a great guy. His confidence and willingness to mentor others was greatly appreciated and played a major role in the team's success.

Big Al was also a part-time agent.

His full-time job was in the role of Fresno County Deputy Sheriff. He was a well respected veteran and very passionate about his career. He was also passionate about the benefits of Aflac policy ownership and felt it was his duty to educate each and every fellow police officer and firefighter in the State of California about its value.

Each week during his time off as a deputy, Alan would make the arduous 4-hour trek from Fresno to Los

Angeles. His time would be spent presenting to potential policyholders, assisting with claims and prospecting for future sales opportunities. His mantra was: *"If I don't know where I'm going to be next week before I start this week, I'm out of business."*

Big Al was the hardest worker that I have ever had the privilege to work with and made tremendous sacrifices in his life to succeed.

In the Aflac world, there are several traditions that are practically sacrosanct. One of these is the quarterly occurrence of "Power Weeks". Originally called 'Push Weeks', they have grown from 8 weeks a year to 16+ weeks a year. They are hard-calendared each year for the final month of each quarter and are designed to focus the entire organization on completing sales.

During my tenure as a district manager, one of my leaders occupied the position of Territory Director. Many levels above me. He was super-focused on these 'push' weeks and was very vocal about the ramifications of its results.

During an awards dinner, Alan's collection of plaques and trophies was greatly enlarged. This was a common occurrence at the time. I was always excited to share these moments with him and very proud of his achievements. The recognition by the state organization always tended to re-invigorate Big Al and reconfirm his commitment.

After the ceremonies were completed, we retreated to the hotel bar for some post-celebratory libations. The Territory Director offered to pay and we gladly accepted.

No mention was made of the awards by the director even when the subject was lightly mentioned. You could feel Al's motivation level decreasing rapidly. It was blatantly obvious. I finally decided it was time to speak up and sing Big Al's praises in front of the Director. Alan deserved it.

I vividly remember the Territory Director's response verbatim: "Well, I don't give a damn about what you do the rest of the year. I only care about what you do during the most important 8 weeks of the year. Let's see what you do during push weeks."

It was as if a balloon was popped. Alan's expression went from crestfallen to obviously upset. It took many months of damage repair to overcome the Territory Director's faux-pax. Obviously, this was a study of what NOT to do!

Most salespeople thrive on Praise, Recognition and Appreciation. Especially amongst peers. A career in sales is tough and can be quite lonely at times. A sense of team disconnection can easily appear leaving the salesperson feeling as if they are adrift on a wide ocean with no other ships in view.

My father would always make it a point to truly understand what exactly motivated his team members. Beyond the obvious financial motivation, there usually is something else. It could vary from subsidizing a hobby to taking a destination vacation. He often joked that, "You can come up with a contest that the winners get an all-expense trip to the Henrico county dump and the Martins (one of the organization's top performer duos who loved to travel) will set all kinds of records to win it!". It could be as simple as letting them know that you recognize their efforts and are proud of them. Usually, recognizing them in front of their peers and family members makes it even better.

P.R.A. - Praise, Recognition and Appreciation.

"If You Have to Demote Somebody, You Gotta Do it on their Turf"

For most managers and leaders, having to make a personnel change is one of the most difficult moves to make. Oftentimes, friendships and bonds have been formed making the separation even more challenging. Regrettably, the odds are very high that the situation will be faced at some point or another.

There are several solid rules that my father steadfastly followed when dealing with this potentially volatile situation. The first has to do with *"cushioning the blow."*

Duane Adams (Jimmy nickname: Doo-Wayne), a former manager that reported to him, has often joked about this first rule. "You know that you're being fired if Jimmy approaches you about another position opportunity that better fits your skillset."

At one time or another, the person possessed the skills, talent and work ethic needed for the position. They were hired for a reason. They may have lost their passion. Failed to change with the market. Had extenuating circumstances beyond their control. It's just the right time for each side to make a change for the betterment of both sides.

By taking the time to search for more suitable opportunities, the person is no longer being placed in a bleak, dire position. Additionally, the organization doesn't lose a valuable resource. The breakup is made smoother. Plus, the manager doesn't look like a jerk!

While we are on the topic of jerks, here is another example of 'leadership - what not to do.' It also reinforces Jimmy's second rule of how to create an amicable separation: *"Never, Ever Blindside Them"*

One of my father's best friends throughout his entire career was Mel Jones (AKA - "The Oil Can"). They were first introduced in the late seventies and rapidly formed a bond. Each was in the role of regional manager in Virginia at the time and shared many adventures together - enough to fill many books!

The two friends had made a pact: when one of them was promoted to the state manager position then the other would accompany and support growing the organization's success. My father was soon promoted and assumed the role of state manager in the potato capitol of the world - Idaho. Upon hearing the good news, Mel's quick response was "So, what day are we headed out?"

Since neither of them knew exactly where Idaho was located, they pulled out a map, plotted their course and made their way west.

Mel Jones and Jimmy. Circa 2000

Their arrival made an immediate impact on the Idaho organization. Sales increased and the team grew quickly. In fact, it was so successful that Jimmy was offered a larger state organization in Texas less than a year after his arrival.

Due to the success in his regional role, Mel was then promoted to state manager. He held this position for several years until he was summoned to meet with the man that he now directly reported to - a newly promoted territory director.

Unconcerned, Mel boarded a flight from Boise to Portland, Oregon, the location of the territory office. His new boss was waiting to greet him at the end of the jetway (in those days, you could actually do that!).

"Well Mel", the director said. "You don't need to come to the office. Thought I'd save you some time and let you know that your services are no longer needed and we are letting you go. Feel free to catch an early flight back."

No warning. No explanation. No sympathy.

A true sign of a weak leader is one that makes politically motivated personnel decisions. One who makes back-room deals when making organizational changes.

True leaders understand the importance of coaching the individual long before a major change such as a demotion is required. If both sides are clear about benchmarks that must be met, then the person is not blindsided and acceptance will be eased.

If a demotion is eminent, my dad felt the bad news should always be delivered in person, face-to-face. Location was also important. *"Always do it at their office. They will feel more comfortable on their own turf."*

An added benefit will be: *"They won't be tempted to tear up anything either!"*

"Waffles are Made to be Eaten"

Inevitably, conflict will arise when a group of competitive individuals work on the same team. Ignoring or brushing these differences of opinions will only increase the level of toxicity. The manager is usually apprised of the situation and is thrust into the role of judge, jury and mediator.

It usually goes something like this:

The manager is approached by one of the feuding parties and are more than eager to inform the manager of the situation. They plead their case, question the character of the offending teammate and finish by asking for some kind of retribution.

Indignant, the other party completely refutes the claims of the first party and disparages the other's ethics.

Both make compelling arguments, however, the truth usually lies somewhere in the middle. The manager is forced to make a decision.

My father was very adapt at diffusing situation such as these.

Fay Martin, one of his longtime managers, used to laugh about it. "You could go into a meeting with Jimmy and the person that you were having issues with and be mad as a hornet beforehand. Next thing you know, we're both happy and going out to dinner together like good old friends that never had a problem!"

What was his key? He made sure to *"let each side tell their sides of the story in front of each other."* There was to be no time limit to the pleadings. Each person could talk as long as they wanted. They were allowed to refute the others comments until an agreement was reached.

"People just want to be heard. They want to be listened to. It's amazing how angry folks can calm down when they're allowed to get things off of their chests."

Once a decision is made and agreed upon, no change will be made. Once a leader makes that determination, they have to stand fast and not cave in to later influences. They cannot waffle. They will be eaten.

IV

"You Gotta Get 'em in the Eyes"

The Jimmy Hill Guide to Selling

I'm not sure if its due to the racing blood that has coursed through his blood or a lack of observing the surroundings while driving but there is one record that I pretty sure my father unofficially holds: He has witnessed the dreaded blue flashing lights in his rearview mirror admonishing him to pull his vehicle to the side of the road more than anyone I have known. If the Guinness Book of World Records included a category for "Most moving violations dismissed by the roadside," Jimmy Hill's record would probably never be challenged.

While most normal folks would experience a feeling of immense dread and impending doom when placed in this type of situation, he simply has viewed these numerous encounters with officers of the law as simply mild inconveniences. He has possessed a knack for convincing State Troopers to literally shred violations. He has a true gift for consistently persuading Deputy Sheriffs to merely reprimand him with an oral warning.

One of these encounters took place on a country road outside of the town of Brookneal, Virginia late one evening. It had been a typical long day of sales calls and he was motivated as usual to make even more sales in order afford the never-ending cost of feeding the 'starving birds' at home. The weather was chilly and Jimmy was running late to an appointment.

Approaching the town, he failed to lower his vehicle speed to a reduced posted speed limit. He wasn't exactly sure how many miles per hour over the new speed limit his vehicle was traveling. The semi-hidden state trooper with a radar gun did.

As the officer approached his '79 Mercury Bobcat, he rolled the window down. He was in luck. The trooper was not wearing sunglasses. His eyes were completely exposed.

"Sir, are you aware that the speed limit is 45 miles per hour in this area? Do you know how fast you were traveling?", the trooper inquired.

Most police officers will attest, the usual responses range from, "Oh no, I didn't see the sign." Or "There is no way I was going that fast. I'm sure that I was going about 40..." These replies are usually met with skepticism typically resulting in the issuance of a moving violation.

With solid eye contact made, Jimmy's response was confident and more, importantly, truthful.

"Yes, I come through here all the time. Not really sure how fast I was going but I'm guessing about 55 to 60 miles per hour."

Taken back a bit, the trooper replied, "Sir, let me get this straight. You are saying that you admit that you were driving at least 10 miles per hour over the posted speed limit? You are aware that this offense can result in me issuing you a speeding ticket along with a fine?"

Continuing to unwaveringly maintain eye contact,

he responded in the affirmative.

"Sir, would you care to explain why you knowingly exceeded the speed limit?"

"Absolutely," he explained. "It's been a long day and I'm running late to an appointment to talk to a couple about some valuable insurance. The construction outside of Bedford held me up. I promised these folks that I would get there at 7pm. I intend to keep that commitment."

"Sir, while I can appreciate that, that still is not an excuse for speeding."

"It's not an excuse. I did recognize there was no other drivers around and given the conditions, it seemed safe. To me, the potential risk of paying a fine was outweighed by my commitment to fulfill a promise."

The officer thought for a moment. Jimmy knew: the trooper's silence was a positive indication that no ticket would be issued.

Jimmy also applied one of his unwavering rules of selling (another Jimmyism): "*He Who Talks First Loses*"

When faced with long moments of silence, the natural inclination is to continue pleading your case, filling the silence with word after word. Silence drives most salespeople crazy! In reality, the person that is being "sold" is simply analyzing the information that they have been presented. They are processing while forming an opinion.

After what probably seemed to be an eternity, the officer was intrigued.

"Sir, what kind of insurance program can be that important?"

"I'm glad you asked. You know as a State Trooper

in the Commonwealth of Virginia you are eligible to enroll in one or more of these valuable programs at a reduced rate. Let me quickly show you how they work but I really need to make it to that appointment.........."

Yes. He not only merely received a warning, but the trooper became a proud policyholder as well. I'm not sure if he made it to the appointment on time though.

What has been the magic secret to speeding ticket avoidance? Being truthful and getting 'em in the eyes! Not literally physically attacking someone's optical organ (quite ironic considering his later misfortunate encounter with a nail gun). It is as simple as looking them in the eye. Making sustained eye contact. Not to the point of creepiness, though!

While the *words* he used may have presented a compelling argument, they still are merely that – words.

Unconsciously, we inherently choose to believe non-verbal communication signs over *words* themselves. If you have participated in any training session or seminar, you have been apprised of this sales psychology nugget. I can still remember being instructed in my first "sales school" to nod my head up and down when requesting affirmation from a potential client. On the flip side: avoiding eye contact, looking down, shaking your head from side to side when "closing a sale" will surely result in a declination. It is basically akin to closing as sale by using the statement - "You don't want to buy this stuff do you?"

Speaking of closing…..

"Don't Call it a Close"

My father has always seemed to grimace when asked about how to close a sale. I asked him about it one time and he explained:

*"The word 'close' itself seems to imply that the door has shut. There is no next step. The relationship has come to an ending. There is finality. Refer to it as the **next step**."*

A great piece of advice on how to make it to the 'next step' in which my father used to impart to many aspiring salespeople was very simple: "As you begin a presentation to a potential client, remember - there is an understanding that there will be a point in the conversation where the customer will be asked if they would like to purchase the product or service. All you have to do is ask So, just *ask*."

I vividly remember him emphasizing the second part of this advice during a training seminar.

"The second key to gaining their commitment is: once you have asked, **SHUT UP!**" as he slammed his hand down on the front row table. I think the first three rows of folks jumped in their seats! "Now is not the time to get **diarrhea of the mouth**!"

He continued, "I've seen more salespeople talk themselves out of a sale by simply not **SHUTTING UP!**"

"Gotta Believe in It to Sell It"

Do you own the product that you are offering? At some point in a salesperson's career, someone will ask this question. Your credibility along with the value of your product or service will surely be questioned if the answer is negative.

Jimmy was adamant about salespeople in his organization owning insurance policies with the company they represented. He taught us to make our clients very aware that we're proud owners by inserting phrases such as: "What attracted me to this policy when I enrolled was this feature...." or "When I filed a claim on my policy, this benefit worked like this...." Subtle, but very effective.

What if the product that you are selling is yourself? People can sense your belief in yourself and your abilities. Confidence, not cockiness, comes with time and experience. These can only be accomplished by *doing*.

"If its to be, I believe in me." - Jimmy Hill

"The Squirrel Hunter is the Fattest, Happiest Hunter of All"

In rural communities, hunting is not only a popular pastime, but serves as a valuable food source for local families. One cannot help but notice the empty halls of the local high school as the first day of hunting season commences each year in the county in which I was raised,

Buckingham.

In my dad's opinion, there are three distinct categories of hunters: 1. The elephant or big game hunter, 2. the deer or wild game hunter and 3. the squirrel or small animal hunter.

The first of these, the elephant hunter, spends large amounts of money in order to attend his hunt. He has to purchase the best hunting equipment. He has to buy expensive plane tickets which take him to exotic lands. He has to hire the services of guides that have local knowledge and experience. It is usually a hefty investment with no guarantees of a successful hunt.

Even if he does 'bag an elephant', it has usually been scarred and beaten up by aggressive predators such as lions and tigers. Additionally, he may have issues actually bringing his trophy home.

The deer hunter usually meets with more success than the elephant hunter. However, he must be patient and cautious for his prey is easily startled. Many forays end empty handed, but when he is successful, there is plenty of food to be had. In fact, there is usually enough to be shared with friends.

The squirrel hunter is the fattest, happiest hunter of them all. He doesn't even have to leave the porch of his house. As he sees his prey pass by, all he has to do is point and shoot. He has honed his skills through years through the practice of aiming at the small, moving targets. He has become a master marksman and his table is never bare.

On days that he actually decides to participate in a deer hunt, he has become so proficient that it seems almost too easy for him.

And there is always the possibility that someday the circus may come to town. An elephant may escape rampaging through the town and the authorities may need some assistance with a tranquilizer gun....

The squirrel hunter story is actually quite ironic. Over the years, Jimmy became known for procuring large clients for Aflac such as the City and County of Los Angeles accounts. However, none of these would have been possible had he not honed his skills 'squirrel hunting' door-to-door down the backroads of rural Virginia.

"People Buy on Emotion. Emotion is Not Always Subject to Logic"

How many times have you taken a shopping excursion with no intentions on buying? When approached by a salesperson, your pat response is "No thanks, I'm just looking." Upon returning home, you proceed to the trunk and remove the bag containing your recent purchase. What just happened? There was no logical reason for you to remove the credit card from your wallet and hand it to the cashier completing the purchase. But yet, you did. Your emotions took over and now you attempt to justify with logic.

During a presentation, Jimmy was known to emphasize points by sharing stories. This method proved to be very effective. His goal was to have them become emotionally invested into the product. He wanted them to *feel* the need for its benefits. However, the story-telling actually contained a dual-purpose.

A vital key that is often missed during the euphoria of a successful sale is the other part of the equation. Invariably, the logical portion of our brain will attempt to intervene when emotions come into play. This sometimes leads to a sense of confusion. The retention of the product is in doubt.

The secondary purpose of this sharing of stories and providing scenarios is to reinforce the initial 'emotional' judgement and placate the skeptical, logic driven portion of the decision making process.

"A 'No' Just May Be a 'No' For Now"

The family's main vehicle failed to pass the state inspection leading to the need for installation of new brake pads. The trusted refrigerator finally conked out. An unexpected family emergency which required the last minute purchase of airplane tickets. Things happen. Usually at the worst possible time.

These unpredictable hits to the family budget can and do occur requiring the proverbial 'tightening of the belt.'

There is an old sales cliche: "It's all about the timing." If a family is in financial distress mode, the odds of them purchasing your product is probably very slim. It has nothing to do with the need for your product or in no way disparages your selling ability. They just simply cannot afford it. At least, for now.

"A 'no' just may be a 'no for now." By respecting the potential client's current situation and reassuring them that things can and will change for the better, the opportunity for a future sale remains wide open.

"Sometimes the Sale is Just Not Worth It"

We've all been in social or business settings when comments are made that seem a bit odd. Statements that you inherently know to be either false or you completely disagree with.

I had received a potential new client lead from a partner insurance broker that looked promising. It was a manufacturing company that employed over 200 employees - all perfect candidates for participation in my insurance programs!

The business was located south of Petersburg, Virginia. As luck would have it, my father had a meeting scheduled in the same vicinity so we decided to share a ride. He agreed to simply observe the meeting and resist the urge to interject comments. This would require difficult restraint on his part given his love of conversation!

As we began the meeting, all seemed well. I was in the zone and the presentation flowed. It doesn't matter how old that we become, we still look for parental approval of our skills. I was crushing it and I'm sure dad could not be more impressed. He had to be proud.

The meeting continued, however I started noticing that some of the comments voiced by the business owner were a bit odd. His perceptions of the health care system were a bit troubling along with his views on employee/employer relationships. The ramblings increased. He still remained interested in the offer, though.

Not wanting my father to witness his prodigy fail to secure the deal, I continued on with the presentation. It became even more bizarre. However, the business owner began to discuss implementation logistics and next steps. The sale was essentially made.

True to his word, my father was amazingly silent throughout the entire encounter. At this crucial juncture, he suddenly decided to speak.

"Well, this has been very informative meeting with you today, but we are running late for our next appointment. We'll contact you after doing a bit of research as to whether we should move forward. Thanks for your time."

He then proceeded to stand up and head to the door without uttering another word.

I was stunned.

I had seen a sure deal suddenly derailed by none other than the sales legend himself - the Jimmy Hill.

As we walked to the car, we both remained silent. I wasn't sure exactly what to say. How was I going to tell the referring broker that my father had just completely blown the deal. Had I somehow disappointed my dad - my mentor?

After a few minutes, he spoke. *"You know, sometimes landing a deal just ain't worth it. That guy was crazy. If he became one of your customers, you will never be able to please him. It would cause you more trouble in the end, he will look at every reason to kick you out....and be very vocal to other businesses and he will try to tell your broker friend that you have shortcomings as a professional. Son, sometimes making that one sale may put some quick money in your pocket, but in the long-run it will be a royal pain!"*

Lesson learned.

"Even D Students Can Make It, Too"

Education, Knowledge, & Self Improvement

Jimmy grew up in the county of Buckingham, Virginia in the 1940's and 50's and was educated through the public schooling system. Little was known at the time about learning theories and how to apply them. Educators tended to take the "one size fits all" approach with little room for deviation based on learning styles and unique student needs.

As mentioned earlier, my father suffered from undiagnosed dyslexia along with a stuttering speech impediment. Unfortunately, his knowledge assessments reflected these liabilities and grades were negatively affected. This landed him in the notorious "D" Row.

Apparently, in those days, teachers physically seated students in rows based on their current grade classifications. Dad would intermittently jump back and forth between the C and D rows, sometimes landing in the F row! Mostly, his days were spent hanging with the D crowd.

Opportunities in a rural community tend to be limited, especially for folks that can barely fulfill the minimum requirements for attendance at their high school graduation and earn their diplomas. The effect that this negative system of student classification had on my father was profound. It placed a chip on his shoulder and created a burning desire for him to overcome this skewed classification.

Yes, even D students can make it, too. He proved it.

"If You Ain't Smart, Get Smart"

You've probably heard the old cliche "Paralysis of Analysis." Over the years, it has proven to be a major hurdle for aspiring salespeople and derailed many hopes, dreams and desires. Many of these folks possess ambition. They have the needed skillsets. They understand the work ethic that is required. But for some reason, they postpone committing to actually make sales calls. Their excuses - I just don't think I'm quite up to speed on everything. What if somebody asks me a question that I can't answer.

Even though his academic career was lacking, my dad absolutely loved to read books. Usually, they were of the 'inspirational' or 'self-help' variety, however, many times he could be seen studying industry magazines and periodicals. He was as happy as a kid on Christmas morning upon discovering what he called, "The Google".

"Have you seen this? You can find anything on this thing. It's amazing!", he exclaimed. We have found ourselves having to temper his enthusiasm from time to time and implore him to insure that the source was credible.

Professionals understand that continued industry knowledge and relevance are vital to gaining client commitment and retention. To some people, this diligence comes naturally. To others, it may be a chore. Whichever category that you feel you relate to, it doesn't matter. It is simply a fundamental part of your sales journey.

"Just Show 'Em How To Make A Living"

My career in sales management was moving along smoothly. I had developed some great partnership relationships and my team had grown. I felt that one of the key ingredients to continued sales growth was developing a high knowledge level by implementing a strong training regimen for my team members.

Noticing our consistently solid results, Jimmy approached me about utilizing our training process for the larger, state organization. At first, I was hesitant. I wasn't confident in the scalability of my system and brought this concern to his attention.

"What exactly would you like for the folks to leave with? I've got a lot of industry information to share. Sales techniques and some really cool stuff about the psychology of selling. Plus, I can add in products, prospecting, handling objections....." I inquired. "There are a ton of things I can teach your new agents!"

He suddenly went into his 'deep thought' mode.

"No. That all sounds great and it's probably things they will need to learn at some point, but I just want one question to be answered when they come out of the class - Can they go out that afternoon and sell an insurance policy and make some money?"

Simplify the process. Actually, it seems easier but it really is quite a bit more difficult to achieve. Usually, the presentations that are the simplest are the most successful.

Several years later, Becky Davis, then Senior Vice President at Aflac, attended one of these "sales schools". The company was in the process of developing a standardized training program across the nation along with establishing a dedicated trainer role. She had received positive feedback from our training and had noticed our high levels of new agent success.

At one point during the class, she inquired about the relatively rudimentary nature of the material.

Jimmy's viewpoint on training has been simple. It's not the trainer's job to convey their own personal level of genius. It's to convey needed information. The more complicated this information becomes, the more difficult it will become for the students to relate with and comprehend. If the new salesperson finds this information too challenging to understand, the ability for them to replicate it will become even more challenging which will dramatically lower their confidence level.

"R2A2"

I could not, in good conscience, leave out the formula that my father has firmly believed has been a guiding light during his career for many decades. He did not invent it. It was not his idea in any way shape or form. But he learned it. He internalized it. He believed in it. He has lived it.

The R2A2 formula was developed by W. Clement

Stone, founder of Combined Insurance and one of my father's mentors along with the famous motivational author, Napoleon Hill (no relation). It deals with observation and application of proven ideas and techniques.

It goes something like this:

The first step is to **Recognize** a proven sales technique, strategy or principle that you could see benefiting you and helping you improve in some way or another. This requires studying your contemporaries and analyzing the things that are making them successful. Once you have ascertained what it exactly is, you must then determine how it can **Relate** to your business, experiences or life in general.

After you have figured out how it can fit into your world, you then should **Assimilate** it into your daily routine. Finally, you should take **Action** until the improved change becomes a habit.

A great example of this was the manner in which every meeting has commenced during his tenure. He recognized the power of positive thinking during his days with Amway and the how it could help with developing a great culture within an organization.

Realizing that an organization's attitude begins with its leaders, he felt that it was important to allow meeting attendees the opportunity to share positive news in their lives with their teammates. This was assimilated into every meeting agenda with attendees anxiously awaiting their turn to contribute their stories.

Jimmy, Margaret and W. Clement Stone. Circa 1977

"There's a Fine Line Between a Yes and a No"

The obligatory sales meeting. You check your calendar and sure enough, it's scheduled for today. Given past participations in these motivational events, you may be less than enthused in attending. Is it worth your time? Should you just bag it and not go? The short answer is 'no'. Just go. However, go with an open mind.

Listen closely to the material presented. Resist the urge to check your emails or play a game on your phone. You may just miss that one vital piece of information. That one piece of advice that may make all the difference in your career. It could be a game changer.

"There's a fine line between a yes and no. A yes can feed you. A no can starve you. Anything that you can

pick up along the way that may just tip the scales and move the needle over to a yes is worth its weight in gold."

It'd be a shame if you missed it because you were consciously inattentive.

VI

"Don't Be an Empty Milk Carton"

Relationships & Longevity

A sense of belonging. A sense of feeling wanted and needed. A longing for respect. A need for appreciated contribution. These are common traits that pretty much everyone shares. Inherently, we have a pack mentality. There are loners, however, they are the exception and not the rule.

We are naturally drawn to the implied safety that a group provides and fear banishment.

In the mid-nineties, we attended yet another seminar featuring upper management. While the meeting had a positive tone for the most part, one speaker stood out and the level of negativity spouted has achieved legendary status amongst our family. It was so memorable that it even became the motivation for another Jimmyism - one that we still consistently recite to this day.

Apparently, the current sales figures were not acceptable to this manager. He ranted continuously and berated all in attendance.

"I don't care about what you did last year, last month or even last week!" he exclaimed. "This team's numbers are pitiful. You all are like used milk cartons. And do you know what I do with used milk cartons? I throw them away because they are no longer needed."

Wow. We didn't expect to hear that.

Not really feeling too good about myself at that point and I'm sure most everyone else in the room were dealing with similar emotions. Our sense of team worth was questioned and our places within the group were now a bit unstable. I didn't want to be thought of as 'used-up' and my thoughts soon drifted to departing this pack and joining another.

We understand the manager's intent to motivate the team to achieve its potential. I'm sure that he felt that by taking this tact, he would maybe light at fire. He may have been a bit delusional as to it bearing positive results. He was mistaken. He was soon demoted and became a used milk carton himself.

What elements are needed for a long career? What mindset should you possess in order to *thrive and not just survive?* How can you avoid becoming **a used milk carton**?

Here are a few Jimmyisms that may assist you on your quest for career and relationship longevity:

"The Test of Time"

"We have just met. I don't know you. You don't know me", my father would announce as the end of a meeting drew near. *"We have both had successful careers and lives and I'm sure they will continue on that path even*

if we never see each other again. But, let's see if we can stand the test of time together. Let's see where we are in two years from now. I'm willing to bet that we'll both be happy that we happened to cross each others paths."

Long term relationships rely on a feeling of trust between both individuals. Trust rarely comes immediately. It blossoms over time.

I have concluded most of my training sessions or seminars by paraphrasing a quote by noted motivational author Brian Tracy: *"Character is the ability to follow through on a decision or commitment long after the excitement of the moment has long passed."* We all have had great initial meetings that are filled with optimistic promise. Both parties are excited. Time passes. Enthusiasm wanes. You know the ending.

This begs the question: *How would you describe your character? Do you find that your relationships stand **the test of time**?*

"The Goosee and The Goosor"

Have you been in a social situation where a fellow attendee is aggressively coaxed into sharing a story? A story that has been told over and over to a delighted crowd. You may have heard it many times, but you look forward to hearing again. It just seems to get better with each retelling.

This would be an apt description for the famous

Jimmyism - "The Goosee and The Goosor". Whether it has been his delivery or the lesson that it imparts, its popularity has never waned throughout the years.

A bit of a disclaimer: For many years, neither my brother, mother or myself had a clue as to what this story actually meant. We were just as confused as everyone else. We still enjoyed its appearance and his great enthusiasm for repeating it as much as everyone else though!

After great study and many interrogatories with my father, I *think* I understand it and I will summon all of my interpretive skills in order to give a somewhat correct explanation.

Essentially, there are two types of people in the the world: the Goos-ee and the Goos-or.

The Goos-ee is proactive in everything they do. They aggressively pursue opportunities and tend to be impatient.

The Goos-or is reactive. They cautiously wait and overly analyze situations justifying their actions with prudence.

In the wild, the Goos-ee eventually will use the Goos-or to achieve their goals. Do you aspire to be a Goos-ee or the Goos-or?

"You Can't Lift Yourself Up By Putting Someone Else Down"

Every company has competitors. Even people within the same companies oftentimes compete against each other for a sale. When placed in a competitive situation, a natural inclination is to make comparisons between yourself, your company, your product, your service and your adversary. There may be a desire paint a negative picture of your challenger while elevating yourself to the heights of perfection. You may want your customer or person that you are trying to convince to have serious seeds of doubt in your competitor and complete faith in you and your capabilities. This approach is completely wrong and usually does more harm than good.

My father offered us a challenge. "Accentuate the positive aspects of your competitor in front of the potential client." This approach serves many purposes and allows you to differentiate yourself.

How? Your prospect will view you in a more favorable light.

One of the negative stereotypes that salespeople are saddled with is the inability to be completely truthful particularly when placed in a competitive situation. By taking the high road, a much higher level of credibility will be achieved.

Another bonus is the ability to display your industry knowledge. You show them that you not only know about your company but about your competitor as well. Clients preferred to deal with experts in their fields. This increases their level of trust in your professional abilities.

One of his professional goals was simple: When appearing at an industry event attended by contemporaries - competitors included, you should ***be able to hold your head proudly, safe in the knowledge that you have conducted your business ethically, morally and gained*** *the respect of your peers. You gotta race 'em clean."*

"Outgo/Income/Upkeep/Downfall"

The year was 1980. Summer had passed and the trees were now bare. We were settled in our newly rebuilt home and dad continued to receive award plaques based on his stellar sales performance. They seemed to arrive every week.

Earlier in the year, he had been promoted to district manager while mom deftly handled the administrative details from the office located in our home. Based on their performance, he soon was approached by Weegie Thompson, the American Family Life State Manager at the time.

"Jimmy, how would you feel about taking over as regional manager for the western part of the state? The office is located in Roanoke and there are some really good folks down there."

Seeing this proposal as a great opportunity to advance in the company, he immediately accepted the promotion. There were, however, three issues that accompanied this assumption of this new position that were not taken fully into consideration.

First, the office was located approximately two and a half hours away from our home. Some parts of the region were over four hours away. Logistical concerns due to this geographical situation required either the relocation of the family to Roanoke or an extreme amount of windshield time on his part.

Secondly, all expenses for the sales operation were to be covered by the regional manager. This included the office rent and all other associated costs. Suddenly, his cost of doing business dramatically increased.

Finally, due to the increased responsibilities of this upper management position, the amount of time that he actually was able to sell policies directly to customers would dramatically be reduced. His compensation would become dependent on the overall sales of the organization. Mr. 'If it's to be, I believe in me' would suddenly have to rely on the efforts of others. This was a major gamble.

Add into the mix, my brother had recently begun his studies at the University of Virginia. Tuition was due. My music career needed funding and the regular bills continued to roll in. Serious decisions had to be confronted.

At first, my parents came to the conclusion that he should simply commute based on family budgetary concerns. He had a cousin that lived in Roanoke. She and her husband graciously allowed him to crash on their couch in the beginning, however, feeling like he was overstaying his welcome, he devised an alternative solution - He began to spend his nights sleeping on the couch in the reception area of the office. Not ideal but *'You've got to do what you have to do. Whatever it takes.'*

Due to his dogged determination and self sacrifice, the sales organization's performance dramatically increased. A winning culture was developed. Corporate management was beginning to take notice of this country guy whose team continued to break sales records.

On the surface, it looked as though we were winning. In reality, we were barely holding on.

Unfortunately, my father was rarely seen around our house in Buckingham and the financial strain could not go unnoticed. Peanut butter and jelly sandwiches appeared for dinner. My brother and I were assigned more tasks around the house in order to replace my dad's contributions. I could see the strain on my mother's face. My parents never let on to us kids how hard things were. They felt we shouldn't have to worry.

Eventually, the commute and his absence from the family took its toll. My brother was gone to college and I was in my final years of school. His hungry little birds were flying away from the nest and he was missing those final, precious days. The decision was made to rent an apartment in Roanoke and for my mother and I to accompany him. The expenses just increased, however, the family's quality of life increased as well.

Fortunately, his efforts and sacrifices did not go unrewarded. Another promotion was soon offered and immediately accepted. He was now handed the reigns of a much larger region with a greater income. Plus, our home in Buckingham was located in the dead center of it!

My father was not fortunate enough to attend business school. He only made it six months in college (he always said he was a fast learner!). Business experiences like those he lived through in Roanoke did give him a Masters in the proverbial 'school of hard knocks', though.

He learned a valuable lesson - *If your outgo exceeds your income, your upkeep becomes your downfall.*

"Don't Chase a Title"

Humans are interesting. Especially salespeople. For many driven people, the perception that others have of them sometimes trumps the common sense decision making process. Too often, career decisions are made based on how they are viewed by their contemporaries versus simple business acumen. Judgements are skewed by lofty aspirations of professional grandeur.

Corporate America has been littered with well-intentioned promotion candidates that suddenly find themselves ill-equipped to handle assigned responsibilities upon receiving an impressive title. All too often, the title suddenly imparts an increased sense of self importance typically resulting in subordinates shaking their heads in disbelief.

Whether the promotion decision may have been politically motivated by superiors or the candidate's interview skills were phenomenal, many of these individuals seem *'to fail forward and are soon promoted out the top'* (yet another Jimmyism). Eventually leaving veterans to ponder "what ever happened to so-and-so? Wow. They really screwed things up." Eventually, the former impressive title-holders are *flushed away* never to be seen again. As Jimmy would say: *"Be patient, they will soon be gone. BS eventually ends up being flushed down the toilet."*

Organizations that are reliant on sales performance to drive profits seem to be particularly susceptible to this practice.

Instead of being blinded by the prospects of colleague adulation, look instead at the actual duties and responsibilities of the role.

Remember: ***"It's not about the title itself. It's about what you 'do' with the title."*** It's really about the *position* and your ability to effectively contribute to the organization and yourself.

If you are approached to accept a new position, be careful in accepting it.

Do you feel that your odds of success in the role are high? Will you be allowed to use your creative energy and knowledge without feeling constrained? Will there be a proper balance between your business and personal lives? Will you enjoy your role? Will you be happy?

"Something of Something is Better Than Something of Nothing"

Greed. The downfall of many aspiring salespeople. Through the years, million-dollar accounts have been lost due to infighting over even the smallest amount of commissions. "Sure-thing" deals have fallen though never to be revived. Once promising careers have come to standstills over a perceived slighting of acceptable compensations.

You can receive the highest commission package, however, if no sales are made because other influential parties are not properly incentivized - no revenues will be forthcoming. This may sound like a 'no-brainer', but *"it is amazing how difficult a concept it seems to be for many folks to grasp."*

Often, I was confused at the 'bargaining' table as I witnessed my father actually negotiating his personal commission percentage *down*. *"As long as I'm included somewhere, I'm fine with that."* It all comes down to volume and duplication of efforts. The more people that are contributing to the overall success of the 'deal', the greater chances for success. The more 'skin in the game' that folks have, they will inevitably become more focused on driving new sales….and, eventually, the retention of the customers.

"Start With Something Good. End With Something Great"

Attending a meeting, seminar, awards dinner, etc. hosted by my father was always an adventure. As mentioned earlier, he was a firm believer in the Walt Disney philosophy: *"Whatever you do, do it well. Do it so well that when people see you do it they will want to come back and see you do it again and they will want to bring others and show them how well you do what you do."*

My mother always played a major role in the

execution of these events. Her nickname of "the hawk" was very fitting as she handled even the smallest of details with ease. She misses nothing!

The dynamic between them throughout the years has always been interesting to observe. He has been the 'Big Picture' thinker while she has assumed the role of the person that puts the puzzle pieces together and connects the dots. His grand ideas are tempered by her budgetary concerns. His attempts at agenda creation are modified by her reality checks.

One area that we all agreed upon: These events must be energetic, positive, and motivational.

As far back as I can remember, our meetings were begun by allowing attendees to share a piece of good news with the audience. (except, of course, the time when Jimmy fired the entire organization in Los Angeles!) It didn't matter if the news referenced business or personal lives, it just had to be good news.

The meetings were adjourned with the audience being prompted to *"always pursue your dreams. Just GO FOR IT!"*

VII

"Lucky Sperm"

Jayisms & Gregisms

The title of this chapter is probably a bit of a head-scratcher, but one of my father's favorite Jimmyisms in his later years actually referenced the reproductive process. It has nothing to do with a jealousy towards privileges gained by simply being born to the right parents. It actually means the opposite. It really applies to folks that squander opportunities based on their misperceived levels of false entitlement due to their genetic makeup.

Character plays a much greater role in success than birthright. ***"Sales is the ultimate equal opportunity employer. Everyone has the same chance."*** Ultimately, their success or failure is dependent on their own attitudes, work ethics, quests for knowledge and skillset.

There are certain characteristics and traits that are handed down from generation to generation. As much as we can resist doing the same things our parents did that annoyed us while we grew up, there seems to be some sort of pre-ordained gene that will force us down that path. I'm far from being a scientist, but I'm sure that the DNA structure we received from our parents plays some sort of role in this. I find myself watching my brother display mannerisms similar to my father. I catch myself reacting to situations exactly like my mother does.

Or could it really be subconscious mimicry on the part of offspring after years of observing their parents in given situations.

Whatever the reason may be, my brother and I have seemed to pick up one of our father's peculiarities. Yes. We have developed our own sayings based on our years of experiential observations and development. We have become the proverbial 'chips off the 'ole block.'

Greg, Jimmy and Jay Hill. Circa 2006

"They'll Never Tell You That Your Baby is Ugly"

My brother Jay is known for his quick wit, an encyclopedic level of knowledge and easy going nature. He had an extremely successful career with Aflac in numerous leadership capacities throughout the country during a span of over 35 years. Countless times, I've heard agents and managers make the comment, "I wish that I had started my sales career earlier." This is a statement that Jay will never be able to make - he passed his insurance licensing exam the day after his 18th birthday.

One of my favorite "Jayisms" is one that I have used in seminars and training sessions for years:

Imagine yourself presenting to a prospective client. You're hitting your stride. Words are flowing and your diction is perfect. Your prospect is displaying all known buying signs and you determine that its the perfect time to ask for commitment.

Inexplicably, they respond with a resounding "No."

No objections. No reasons given. You are stunned. You need an explanation. You must know why this person made the decision to not precede with your offer. In your opinion, its a no-brainer. They just witnessed a presentation that bordered on perfection. You need answers.

Sales is simply communication. Acceptance of your product or service is determined by their *perception* of the satisfactory fulfillment of a need or desire.

It may be something as simple as their attention distracted on another issue. They may have been annoyed with your presentation style. They may not like your product.

The thing is: They don't have to explain. Sometimes they just don't want to tell you that they feel ***"that your baby is ugly."*** Applying makeup to your baby or even plastic surgery will not change the situation.

Sometimes a "no" is simply that. A No. Pack up and move on to the next customer.

Which segues us to another Jayism.....

"Sales is Simply a Numbers Game"

For many years, eager new salespeople have inquired: "What is the *golden* close?" or implored to divulge "the hidden secret" during training sessions. It's not a secret. It simply comes down to the more people that you see, the more people you will sell.

If you were to stand in the middle of Times Square in New York City during the busiest time of day and ask each passerby, "Would you like to buy an insurance policy?" Eventually, somebody will say, "Yes, I'd like to know more."

You can have the greatest product in the world. You can have the most amazing presentation skills known to mankind. These are completely useless without someone to talk to.

"You're not 007. Don't be a Secret Agent"

Cue the theme song: "Dom-Dee-Dee-Dee—Dom-Dom-Dom-Dom-Dee-Dee-Dee-Dee—Dom-Dom-Dom....." Bond. James Bond. Debonair. Dangerous. Exciting. A man of mystery and intrigue.

My brother and I have always been fascinated with the James Bond character and have reveled in his exploits throughout his movies and books. We were on the edge of our seats as he narrowly escaped the clutches of the evil Dr. No. We jealously admired his international exploits as he jet-setted around the globe.

For many years, we have anxiously anticipated the arrival of the latest sure-fire blockbuster film. So much so, if fact, we have not missed an opening day viewing of a James Bond movie since 1981! It has become a great tradition for us that I'm sure will continue for many years to come.

Have you ever wondered: How do you think James Bond's neighbors view him? Do they gossip about this guy who rarely occupies his residence and is very secretive about his currently employment status? Their curiosity has to be extremely high!

Imagine if James Bond's income was completely reliant on his ability to transparently persuade potential customers into purchasing a product. What if these sales were predicated on prospecting limited by a cloak of secrecy? I would gamble that the odds of his success would be relatively low. He would probably be forced to downgrade to economy seats on his next international adventure.

Don't be a secret agent in your neighborhood. Let your acquaintances in the community know exactly what you do for a living. Potential prospects from a relationship are invariably yield the best results.

"It's Easier to Birth a Baby Than to Raise the Dead"

All too often, veteran insurance agents seem to develop a crippling disease known as "Renewalitis". Its effect on the organization can be devastating. Decreasing new sales and suspicious guarding of accounts can be repercussions. Frustrated managers find themselves banging their heads trying to reinvigorate these veterans.

Unfortunately, some agents with amazing potential just seem to underperform – they fail to meet initial lofty expectations and eventually fail in the sales industry. Well intentioned managers cajole and attempt to inspire these washouts with little success.

What should a manager do when faced with these scenarios? Sometimes, it's best to just move on for the betterment of both parties and prospect for new talent. It may be the time to "birth a baby."

A sales organization that is not continually growing will eventually wither away and die. Having a constant influx of new talent can work miracles for the immediate and long-term results for a sales team. The enthusiasm and spirit that newly recruited team members bring can be a much-needed jolt to drive new opportunities and may reinvigorate the veterans that may have become jaded, stale or afflicted with "Renewalitis."

"Sometimes You Have to Get OUT of Your Comfort Zone to Get IN To Your Comfort Zone"

Change. You can like it or you can hate it. You can accept it or you can fight it. It can present opportunities or it can produce roadblocks. There is no disputing the fact, however. Change will occur. It must. To quote the character Don Draper from the show Mad Men, "Change is neither good or bad: it simply is."

In the mid to late 1980's, my job was pretty simple. I only had two policy options to present to potential clients. They could be offered to be either billed directly to a policyholder or deducted from an employee's paycheck if their boss was amenable to that arrangement. The applications were less than a page long and the additional paperwork was minimal.

Suddenly, the difficulty level of my job ratcheted up dramatically. During a payroll enrollment alongside a health insurance broker in Chino, California, I was introduced to a concept that changed my relatively easy profession. The broker suggested that we implement a plan utilizing a tax savings strategy based on the IRS code, Section 125.

Huh?

Up until this point in my career, I was completely clueless about anything that remotely dealt with taxes. I would try to save my business receipts, forward them to my tax accountant and usually stare at him blankly when he offered tax advice.

Now, in order to remain relevant in my chosen field, I would be forced to actually learn something about some sort of tax code, inform my clients about it and, hopefully, not get anybody in trouble with the IRS. I was petrified!

My father and his partner, Bill Krzciok saved the day. They were fortunate enough to meet a man named Jack Lutz who actually was an expert in this field. He simplified the process for us and went on to establish Aflac's FlexOne department bringing this valuable tool for agents to use across the nation.

Over time, I became well-versed in Section 125 and it became second nature to me. It became my new comfort zone.

Change. It will come. Many times. Adjusting to it will be uncomfortable at first. Not adjusting to it will be even more uncomfortable.

"Look for the Tell"

A mastery of the game of poker will probably never happen for me. It's just not in the cards (badoom-ching!). Given my challenges with all things mathematical, it has always seemed confusing to me. Trips to Vegas and impromptu poker sessions held in basements amongst friends usually results in my relegation to the role of simple observer.

One aspect of poker that has always intrigued me is the finer art of secretive bluffing and the close observation for the elusive "tell." A tell in poker is a change in a player's behavior or demeanor. It could be a slight involuntary, physical movement that they are unaware of. The tell may give a clue to that player's assessment of their hand. Basically, it's a tip-off.

There are *tells* during the sales process as well: a nodding of the head, a leaning forward, specific questioning about a feature of the product. They are the buying signs that indicate interest. Savvy salespeople are constantly looking for them. They understand that flexibility in a presentation is vital and are not tempted to continue rambling about more and more benefits of their product. They've learned to execute the deal.

"Too many salespeople have talked themselves out of a sale by not simply shutting up and getting the paper signed!" - Jimmy Hill

What if a tell is misread? For example: The client is leaning back in their chair with arms crossed. Bad sign, right? Probably little interest so the odds of a deal are very low. Not necessarily. This could simply be a display of introspection It could be their unconscious demeanor based on more introverted personality type.

What if they seem impatient? They just seem to want the presentation to finish. Again, it could just be their personality type. *"Don't bore us, get us to the chorus!"* Top salespeople are clued-in and realize they should escape from the weeds and discuss higher level benefits.

Too often, inexperienced salespeople are taught to 'stick to the script' with no room for deviation. Script memorization is fine - to a point. The internalization of a proven script can be very powerful and can play a major role in boosting confident levels, however, it must not sound canned or fake.

The real key is simply paying attention and the recognition of the *tell*.

VIII

"Walking Down the Road Talking to Yourself"

The Conclusion of a Legendary Career

My father's father, Roy Sr., was known by many as the "Bulldog". He was a self-taught contractor with a 6th grade education and had a few adages himself. I'm pretty sure that his sayings received the dreaded "eyeball rolls" from my dad and uncles when he communicated them.

As the owner of a successful construction company, he was constantly faced with the difficult task of hiring and firing blue-collar workers. His company's solvency depended on it. He was notoriously firm about his decisions and was not known for a being a tactful conversationalist in this capacity. This is evidenced by his referring to the ending of an employer/employer relationship as *"sending them down the road talking to themselves."*

The "Bulldog" and Jimmy. 1960's

My father's career ended in 2012 as he finally decided that retirement was deserved. Spending time with the family, finishing numerous projects and starting a fudge-making business would all serve to occupy his hours. Unfortunately, the physical stress of manufacturing the candy proved to be too difficult for his aging body.

Subsequent years would find him making appearances at the office. His curiosity with the state of his former company, however, never waned and he could often be heard inquiring, "How are the figures looking? Gonna make quota?"

"Go For It"

The final Jimmyism is probably the most profound. It is brilliant in its simplicity. It is powerful in its application. It is the one that has probably influenced and positively impacted more people during the many decades that my father repeated it.

Early in his career, my father received a simple desk plaque. Each letter was carefully cut out and its face was covered with a blueish, mirror. The chosen font indicated a late 1970's manufacture. It was inscribed with the saying: "**Go For It**".

We are unsure of exactly who presented it to him, but we do know that it was prominently displayed on his desk throughout his career.

When the belongings of his office were finally moved to the storage area of his "dog house" at home, the plaque was relegated to an existence in a cardboard box bound with packing tape.

Jimmyisms have continued to make appearances in conversations over the years. We've respectfully laughed about them and my mother has often said, "We should really write those down sometime before we forget them. They might do some good for somebody in the future." We all nod our heads in agreement and say "Sure thing. We really should."

Life has a funny way of throwing obstacles in the way. Even the best intentions to complete a task seem to be diverted by more pressing matters. Unless it is your profession, writing a book usually falls lower and lower on the 'to do' list. Excuses of inadequacy, dreaded thoughts of negative criticism hurled by faceless individuals along with the mistaken perception that 'there is plenty of time to complete it' all contribute to the postponement of its creation.

But then, there is that simple desk plaque. For so many years, it has stared you in the face. It has reminded you. It has begged you. It has nagged you. *"Go For It!"*

All right dad. Here we go. I'm finally listening. I'm taking your advice. Maybe you are smart after all. Kinda.

When self-doubt creeps in and the inevitable debate whether to pursue an opportunity ensues, ask yourself: "What is the worse thing that could happen. Failure? Well, life is full of failures. One thing, however, is guaranteed: If you don't Go For It - the outcome of the opportunity will not be one of success!"

Time will exact a toll on a person's physical body. Life is finite. History is and will be filled with progressive thinkers, difference makers and mentors that are more than eager to share their experiential wisdom.

Which brings us back to that other plaque that resides in Columbus, Georgia.

Hopefully, that smallish plaque honoring sales leadership pioneers like Jimmy Hill will remain safely in its place, tucked away in that corner of the foyer in the Aflac office tower. Eventually, we will no longer have the advantage of being able to directly reach out to these folks and learn their lessons first-hand. It will be up to us and future generations to seek out and apply their wisdom. Hopefully, we'll refer back to these Jimmyisms.

Let's just try to resist the urge to *roll our eyes, though*....

The Hill Family, Emerald Isle, NC. 2012

About the Author:

Greg D. Hill is a sales veteran, leader, author, motivational speaker and master trainer. Beginning his sales career in 1986, he has garnered many awards and accolades throughout his illustrious career. As an accomplished musician and songwriter, he has travelled extensively around the world and joined the million-miler club.

In addition to membership in the Aflac Pioneers Club, he was one of the original state training coordinators mentoring thousands of agents and managers throughout the years. As founder of the Royal Rum Society and a Certified Master Rummelier, he enjoys promoting the finer art of spirit appreciation. He attended James Madison University, University of Richmond and is a graduate of the Rapport Leadership Institute. He resides in Midlothian, VA with his wife, Liza, and children, Monroe and Marshal.

www.ingramcontent.com/pod-product-compliance
Lightning Source LLC
Chambersburg PA
CBHW071321220526
45468CB00001B/460